Dave Berry

All There Is To Know

Published by Heron Publications Ltd, 2010.

www.heronpublications.co.uk

www.cryinggame.co.uk

For Mariella

...and with special thanks to
Jo and Sue, wherever you are

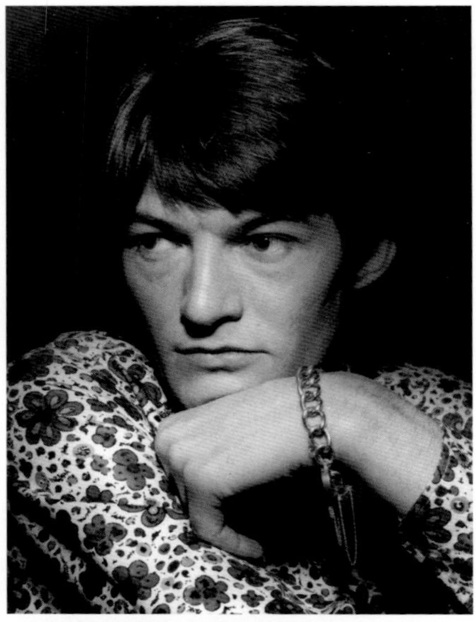

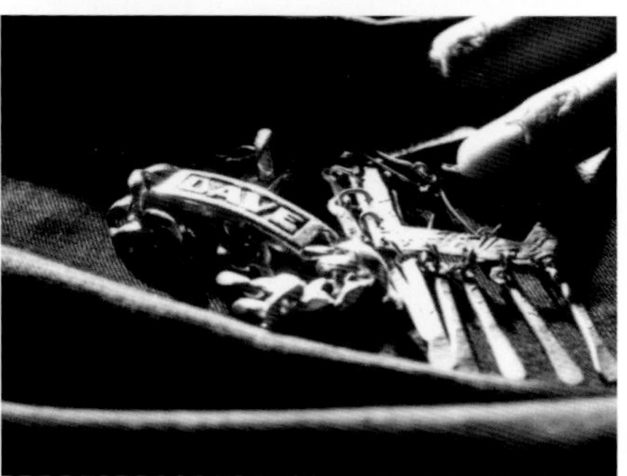

First published in 2010 by Heron Publications Ltd,
24 Hutcliffe Wood Road, Beauchief, Sheffield, S8 0XY.
Telephone: 0114 2357777

www.heronpublications.co.uk www.cryinggame.co.uk

ISBN 978-0-9564825-0-1

Typeset and Designed by Heron Publications Ltd.
Design: Helen Firth
Proof reading: Steve Stewart.

Printed by Printability 2000, Chesterfield, Derbyshire.

Thanks to the following copyright holders for granting permision to reproduce cuttings and images in this book: Sheffield Newspapers, Derbyshire Times, South Yorkshire Times, Seaman Photography Ltd, Active8 magazine, Dronfield Eye magazine, Harry Goodwin, Steve Gullick, Brian and Ashley Yeates.

The authors and publishers have made all reasonable efforts to contact copyright holders for permission to use images and apologise for any omissions or errors in the form of credits given. Corrections may be made in future printings.

Front cover picture: Harry Goodwin.

Back cover picture: Brian and Ashley Yeates.

Track Listing

HITPARADE

JANUARI 1966

Nr.	Titel	Artiest	Vorige	Label	
1	WE CAN WORK IT OUT/ DAY TRIPPER	the Beatles	—	Parlophone	(106)
2	HERE IT COMES AGAIN	Fortunes	3	Decca	(105)
3	YESTERDAY	the Beatles	2	Parlophone	(105)
4	GET OFF OF MY CLOUD	Rolling Stones	1	Decca	(106)
5	WASTED WORDS	Motions	9	Havoc	(106)
6	YESTERDAY MAN	Chris Andrews	—	Vogue	(105)
7	SHAME AND SCANDAL	Shawn Elliott	5	Roulette	(104)
8	STRANGE EFFECT	Dave Berry	4	Decca	
9	A WELL RESPECTED MAN	Kinks	33	Pye	
10	I'M GONNA TAKE YOU THERE	Dave Berry	—	Decca	(105)
11	EVE OF DESTRUCTION	Berry Mc.Guire	6	R.C.A.	
12	YOU'VE GOT YOUR TROUBLES	Fortunes	14	Decca	
13	VARKO STO GIALO (PINDA PINDA)	Hellenique	—	C.N.R.	
14	HELP	the Beatles	11	Parlophone	(102)
15	LA ZORBA	Hellenique	12	C.N.R.	(102)
16	MY GENERATION	Who	—	Polydor	(106)
17	LITTLE THINGS	Dave Berry	—	Decca	
18	CADILLAC	Shamrocks	19	Polydor	
19	CAPRI C'EST FINI	Hervé Vilard	15	Mercury	
20	SOPHIETJE	Johnny Lion	10	Philips	(102)
21	POSITIVELY 4TH STREET	Bob Dylan	—	C.B.S.	(105)
22	YOU'VE GOT TO HIDE YOUR LOVE AWAY	Silky	—	Fontana	
23	CAN I GET IT FROM YOU	Dave Berry	7	Decca	(106)
24	LOVE IS STRANGE	Everly Brothers	16	W.B.	
25	SATISFACTION	Rolling Stones	8	Decca	(103)
26	EARLY BIRD	Andre Brasseur	—	Palette	
27	I'LL GO CRAZY	Phantoms	25	Omega	
28	ALS IK DE GOLVEN AAN HET STRAND ZIE	Ria Valk	23	Fontana	
29	I GOT YOU BABE	Sonny - Cher	17	Atlantic	(103)
30	IL SILENZIO	Nini Rosso	20	Stibbe	(102)
31	LOOK THROUGH ANY WINDOW	Hollies	21	Parlophone	
32	STILL I'M SAID	Yardbirds	—	Riviera	
33	HANG ON SLOOPY	Toy's	22	Stateside	(105)
34	BABY-BABY-BALLA BALLA	Chubby Checker en de maskers	—	Artone	(105)
35	PEOPLE	Barbara Streisand	24	C.B.S.	
36	PLEASE GO	Golden Earrings	13	Polydor	
37	BABY DON'T GO	Sonny - Cher	28	Reprise	
38	UNCHAINED MELODY	Righterious Brothers	—	Metronome	
39	UNIVERSAL SOLDIER	Donovan	26	Pye	(104)
40	WOOLY BULLY	Sam the Sham	38	M.G.M.	(101)

M.P.'s HITPARADE HANGT TWEEMAAL PER MAAND BIJ JE PLATENDEALER !

Europa's grootst
muziekblad voor
tieners en twens

POSTBUS 117, HILVERSU

Introduction

A rare colour picture of Dave and his early band members

BEING too young to remember Dave Berry in his pomp, my first recollection of him dates back to 1968 when my mother returned home from a Women's Institute Christmas Fayre with a smile on her face and an autographed picture of the pop star who had officially opened the event.

His name next cropped up when, looking through some newspaper archives, my eye was attracted to an article from the early 1960s about a singer who had been banned from entering the Carlton Club in Chesterfield because he wore jeans and looked like a beatnik.

So just who was this entertainer who could wow the WI, yet upset the establishment? I was to find out when I started out as a journalist in Dave's local patch and became a frequent visitor to his Derbyshire home in search of stories. During one interview in 2009, with Dave in his fiftieth year as a professional entertainer, I asked when people could look forward to reading his life story.

"Do you think anyone would be interested?" was his rather modest response.

Within a matter of days, two large blue boxes overflowing with press cuttings, magazine articles, publicity pictures, engagement diaries and fans' scrapbooks had left Dave's house for mine and work on this book was well under way.

Dave's career memories are mostly crystal clear and the beauty of this particular life story is that all his anecdotes are backed up by newspaper headlines and photographs. And whenever he talks of characters like Joe Cocker or Bill Wyman, it is most certainly not a case of name-dropping as these people have been his friends and work-mates for half a century.

Everyone I have spoken to about Dave has remarked on the great pride he has always taken in his music, particularly on stage where he has maintained consistently high standards over such a lengthy timescale. Can it really be true that 2010 will see him performing in a seventh decade?

Collaborating with him on this book has been a delight and I hope his army of followers agree that *Dave Berry - All There Is To Know* does justice to the first fifty years of his amazing career.

Yes, Dave, I do think people will be interested in reading your story.

Mike Firth

Musical Youth

I HAVE few memories of my childhood; it's as if I was born at 15. Pop music was invented around the same time and we were meant for each other.

What I do recollect from my youth is that I grew up in a house which was generally buzzing with lively music. My dad, Arthur Grundy, was a semi-professional drummer with The New Mayfair Dance Band, a regular attraction at The Lyric Ballroom in Dinnington, near Rotherham.

We had the *Melody Maker* newspaper delivered every Friday morning to our working class home in the village of Woodhouse, on the Yorkshire-Derbyshire border, and in those days the publication featured jazz stories.

Count Basie "78s" were played on our gramophone and at weekends dad would invite fellow band members to our house for a cup of tea or coffee after their performance; dances were not late in finishing in the 1940s and early 1950s. I remember being in bed and hearing their conversations about music drifting up the stairs to my room.

On holiday in Bridlington and already preparing to make waves

Dad had been performing at The Lyric the night before I was born and, growing up, I was always made to feel that I was a part of his dance band. I was very young indeed when I made my stage debut, sitting alongside him as he played the drums at the Endowed School, Woodhouse.

Later on, he took me to see some of the best jazz and dance bands around, such as The Ted Heath Band. All the big bands seemed to have three vocalists and I suppose they were the "pop stars" of their day.

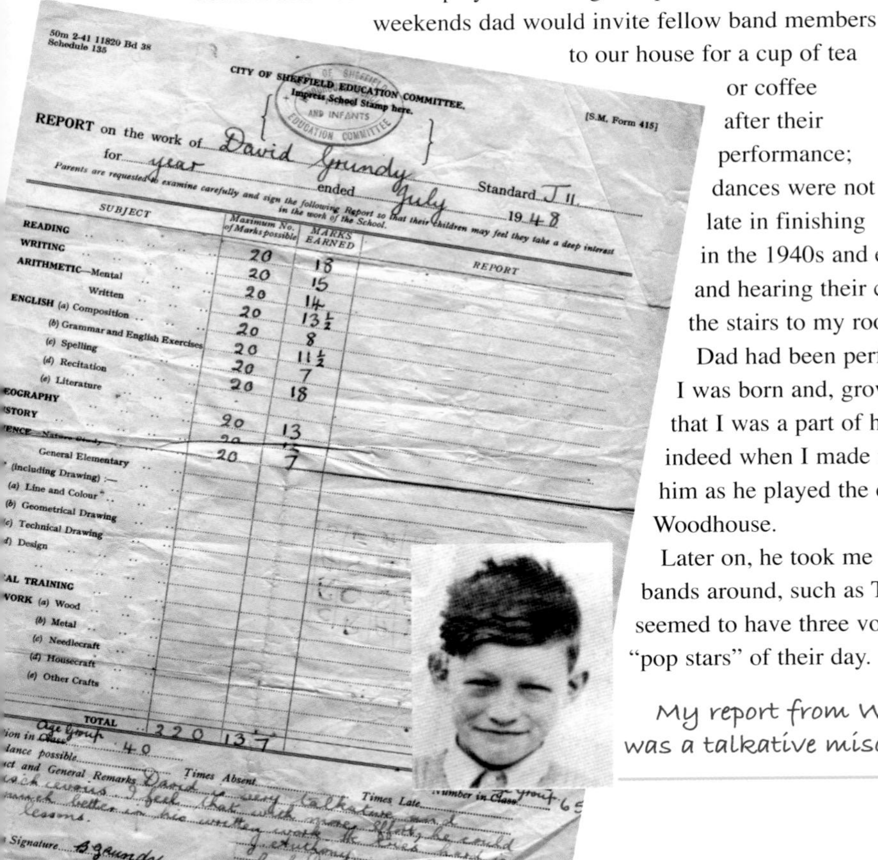

50m 2-41 11820 Bd 38
Schedule 135

CITY OF SHEFFIELD EDUCATION COMMITTEE. [S.M. Form 415]

(Impress School Stamp here.) AND INFANTS — EDUCATION COMMITTEE

REPORT on the work of David Grundy
for year ended July 1948 Standard J II

Parents are requested to examine carefully and sign the following Report so that their children may feel they take a deep interest in the work of the School.

SUBJECT	Maximum No. of Marks possible	MARKS EARNED	REPORT
READING			
WRITING	20	18	
ARITHMETIC—Mental	20	15	
Written	20	14	
ENGLISH (a) Composition	20	13½	
(b) Grammar and English Exercises	20	8	
(c) Spelling	20	11½	
(d) Recitation	20	7	
(e) Literature	20	18	
GEOGRAPHY	-		
HISTORY	20	13	
SCIENCE—Nature Study	20	[illegible]	
General Elementary	20	7	
(including Drawing):—			
(a) Line and Colour			
(b) Geometrical Drawing			
(c) Technical Drawing			
(d) Design			
PHYSICAL TRAINING			
HANDWORK (a) Wood			
(b) Metal			
(c) Needlecraft			
(d) Housecraft			
(e) Other Crafts			
TOTAL	220	137	

Position in Age Group 40 Number in Group 65
Attendance possible Times Absent Times Late

Conduct and General Remarks: David is very talkative and ... I feel that with more effort he could ... better in his written work ... lessons.

Parent's Signature B. Grundy
J. Anthony Class Teacher
Head Teacher

My report from Woodhouse School says I was a talkative mischief at the age of seven

My father Arthur Grundy was a semi-professional drummer and a huge influence on me

With hindsight, I realise how fortunate I was to receive such an introduction to the world of music, a business which was to provide me with international fame in the 1960s and one which has given me a fantastic career and lifestyle for more than fifty years.

There was no overnight *X-Factor*-style success for me; I was one of the original British pop idols and record sales and fame arrived after several years of hard work touring up and down the country.

People tell me I always stood out from the crowd and I suppose I was quite an exhibitionist. I loved to dance but in the mid-1950s pop music simply hadn't been invented in this country. When I wanted to jive I had to wait until the dance band played a samba and even then I was told to go away and do my revolting dance in the corner. To me, rock and roll was the living end and I was thrilled by Elvis Presley. I was a real Sheffield youth, dancing in the aisles like a nut at the cinema during the *Rock Around The Clock* film.

Pictured outside the family home at Beighton, Sheffield

I was fortunate that my mother Bessie and two devoted fans, Jo and Sue, kept detailed scrapbooks of my career from the late 1950s onwards. Every newspaper headline and every magazine picture was painstakingly cut out and sellotaped into volume after volume and now these bulging books are wonderful reminders of those exciting times. However, the very first newspaper stories written about me were not connected with my voice at all - they were all about my dancing exploits.

Whenever the fairground came to town I would be there, at Beighton, Woodhouse or Norfolk Park, but not only for the rides. Just like in the David Essex film *Stardust*, the fairground was a place to experience the latest music and I was always keen to enter the dance contests.

Rock 'n' Roll Champion for Beighton?

Eighteen-year-old David Grundy, 1 Robin Lane, Beighton, a coke oven worker at Brookhouse, is a keen exponent of rock 'n' roll. He is the "star" of regular sessions at Beighton Youth Club and now he has the chance of wider fame. Next month he is to take part in the finals of a national rock 'n' roll championship to be held in London. Pictured above, he is seen practising at a Youth Club session on Tuesday with his regular partner, 17-year-old Maureen Smith, of 6 Woodhouse Crescent. But his partner in the London contest will be a Rotherham girl, Betty Lynn, aged 18, whom he met while on holiday this year. They entered the early rounds of the competition and were successful. Now they are in the finals and should they win, the prize is a fortnight's free holiday in Paris. But David realizes that he and his partner will have to overcome very stiff opposition to become champions and he is not super-optimistic of their chances.

Rock 'n' Roll is here to stay at Beighton Youth Club and I'm in the South Yorkshire Times with my dancing partner Maureen Smith

I would dance to the rock and roll music of Elvis, Bill Haley and Chuck Berry. American jive was the new dance of the time but goodness knows how anyone over here learned how to do it properly because apart from the film *The Girl Can't Help It* none of us would have seen it performed anywhere and there was no-one to give us lessons. With me, I suppose it was all down to having a natural instinct and, being the son of a drummer, the beat must have been in my bones.

Throughout Beighton and Woodhouse I became known as a good dancer and a number of other young people looked up to me even in those early days. I won a rock 'n' roll dance contest at Butlins, Filey, and had my picture in the local papers.

I had no fear of being ridiculed, just a great feeling that comes at that time of life when you are young and don't have to knuckle under to satisfy the man in a suit in an office somewhere. Most people who succeed in music have enjoyed absolute freedom at some stage, getting on with what they choose to do with no fear of the consequences.

My first job when I left school at 15 was as an apprentice fitter and welder with United Coke and Chemicals at Brookhouse, close to my home in Woodhouse. Part of my electric welding and metallurgy training was carried out at Sheffield College's Pond Street building in the centre of the city.

John Lennon once remarked that he had been a well-known local character even before he became a musician. I suppose it was much like that with me because I was different to other people and my work-mates were aware of my interest in dancing and music.

I had to be up early for work every day and at 5.30am I made a point of tuning in to the American Forces Network radio station, broadcasting from Frankfurt in Germany. The reception was crackly and it often broke up altogether but the channel gave me my introduction to rhythm and blues music through American artists such as Smiley Lewis, Chuck Berry and Lewis Jordan.

I played my dad's drums originally, but I was always attracted to the vocal side. There was never a time when I thought "right, I'm going to be a singer", it was more a case of it feeling natural for me to move in that direction and stand in front of the microphone. It wasn't all music though; I was also a keen footballer and played in goal for Beighton Youth Club in the East Derbyshire League.

When I was 16 or 17 I teamed up with my friend Malcolm Green, who owned a guitar, and another pal, John Lomas. We listened to songs by The Everly Brothers and Buddy Holly and Malcolm and I discovered that our voices had a natural harmony. We won a singing competition in August 1958 at The Locarno in Sheffield and were thrilled when we finished runners-up in the national finals in Manchester.

With my tie tucked neatly into the top of my trousers, I pose with Dominoes colleague Malcolm Green

I could quite easily have had a very different stage name. My grandfather had worked at the Co-op at Woodhouse and when the store had a delivery of sacks of sugar it was his job to look after them all. Most people knew him as "Sugar". My father was given the same nickname and then it was passed on to me.

Whenever I went anywhere like the local pictures, people would recognise me and there would be a roar of "Sugar" from the audience. One of my very first singing performances was at the Cumberland's Head in Beighton, near Sheffield, and the sign outside promoting the event simply read "Sugar in the Evening".

Malcolm, John and I called ourselves The Dominoes but we were soon down to just two spots when John left. The first venue we played was a pub in Worksop. We nervously stood in the corner of the room, Malcolm with his guitar and me playing drums and also singing. It was a most peculiar line-up, but we didn't know any better at the time because there were no guidelines for us to follow. We were together for six or eight months, earning about fifteen shillings a night, and although we never actually decided to finish playing

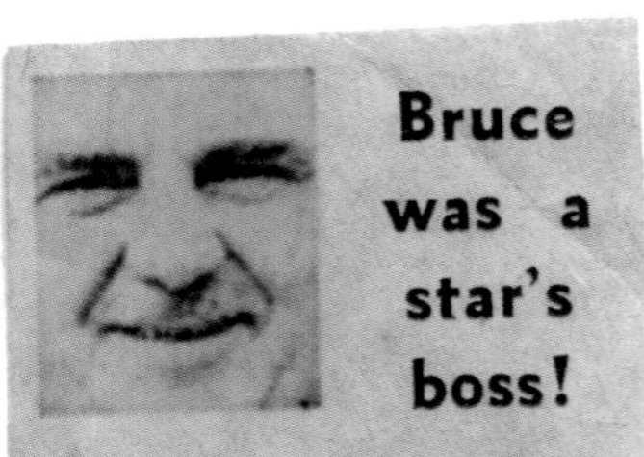

Bruce was a star's boss!

MR. Bruce Green, of West Street, Beighton, used to be pop singer Dave Berry's boss.

He remembers when Dave was an apprentice welder under him at T. W. Wards at Beighton.

"He was 18 then and a good lad. But his ambition was to be a pop star and I used to take him round the pubs at night where he would sing.

"The late nights did not affect his work because he knew where his money at that time came from. He was a happy lad, always smiling at his work — and of course singing."

I was remembered as a happy, smiling welder

D. Grundy, custodian with Beighton Youth Club FC and shown here once again in the South Yorkshire Times

SOUTH YORKSHIRE TIMES, SAT

SEEN BEFORE THE NORTH-EAST DERBYSHIRE YOUTH CLUBS' SEMI-FINAL at Drakehouse Lane playing fields are members of Beighton Youth Club football team: (Back row), B. Owen, B. Penrose, D. Grundy, T. Webster, G. Fewkes; (front row), A. Hinchliffe, D. Fitzackerley, B. Batham, N. Jackson, G. Brocklehurst and D Eyre. (R3299)

together, we just stopped when the bookings dried up.

I was in the papers again thanks to local reporter Bryan Longworth who wrote about the size of my feet. It was probably the first interview I ever gave and the story was all about how difficult it was for me to find suitable shoes for performing in. I wore size 12s from the age of 14 and the report in the *Sheffield Star* in September 1960 said I was spending £6 or £7 a time on new pairs of shoes.

Several other publications followed up the story and the headlines read "Beat in his feet" and "A rocker on his uppers." Getting such publicity in the Press, even if it was all to do with my big feet, certainly added to me becoming rather a familiar character locally. Bryan was the first journalist I had ever met - I don't think I knew what one was until then - and he went on to get stories about me published in the national papers too.

I always had a good relationship with the Press and it was clear to me from the outset that we could help each other; reporters were looking for stories for their newspapers and magazines and people in the public eye like myself were delighted to get all the publicity we could.

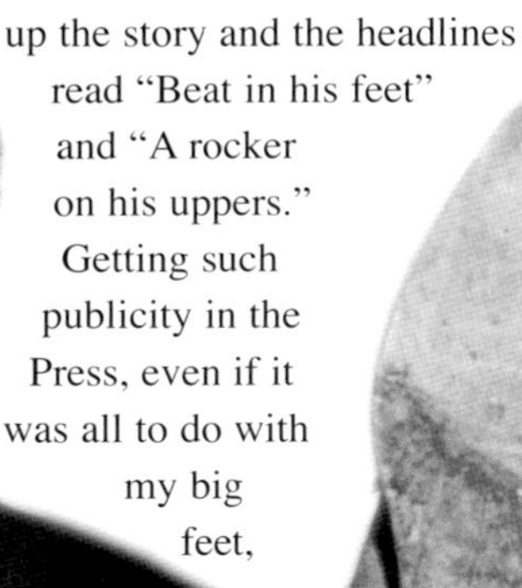

I attracted media interest from the outset... or at least my large feet did

Snapshot of a fresh-faced performer on stage and evidence of me following my dad's passion for percussion

All smiles as I try out my very first electric razor

Cruising

Perhaps the first picture of Dave Berry and The Cruisers on stage. I'm shown here at The Fox, Beighton, with Alan Taylor, John Fleet, Ray Cuffling and Frank Miles

DURING my time with The Dominoes I had simultaneously appeared with The Chuck Fowler Band which had regular bookings at Beighton Cinema and The Cock Hotel at Ripley in Derbyshire. Chuck, who had the inspirational idea to name himself after the American performer Chuck Berry, was the vocalist and very much leader of the band. When he announced he was leaving to join the Army, I found myself in a discussion one Saturday with his remaining band members in the Red Lion pub, next door to the Sheffield City Hall venue. They suggested re-forming the band with me as lead vocalist.

The original group line-up was lead guitarist Frank Miles, his friend John Fleet from Killamarsh on piano and bass, my neighbour from Beighton, Alan Taylor, on second guitar, and drummer Ray Cuffling, also from Beighton. They adopted stage-names; John was known as Red Fleet, Frank was JP Nelson and Alan called himself Wilson Shane.

Cliff Richard had his Shadows, Marty Wilde was

backed by The Wildcats and we picked the name The Cruisers. We thought it would project an exciting American-style image of young men cruising along in the sunshine in their Chevrolets looking to pick up girlfriends. And there we were, playing the pubs of Sheffield, Rotherham and Worksop!

Another early picture with The Cruisers... and where did we get those ties?

We shared an interest in the exciting new sounds which were sweeping over from America; British music of the time was just one step up from the old variety shows. We were fortunate to be able to see some of our heroes when they toured and performed at the City Hall. I saw Buddy Holly and The Crickets there in 1958, just a few months before Buddy was to die in an air crash, but they were a big disappointment to me. There were only three of them on stage - a bass player, drummer and Buddy on guitar and vocals - and, although their music was fine, they

Meeting Gene Vincent (right) on his visit to Sheffield to play at The Gaumont Picture House

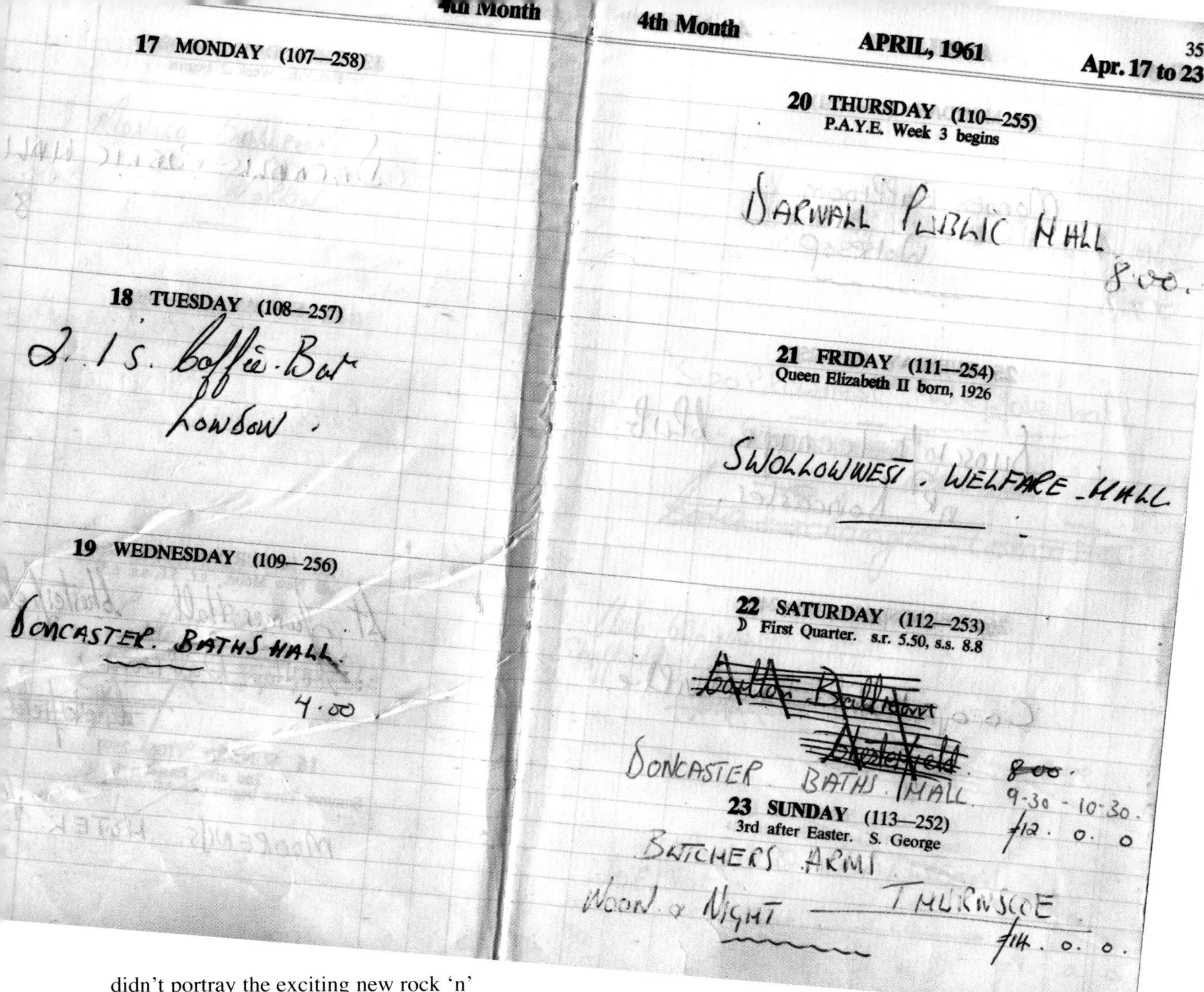

4th Month

17 MONDAY (107—258)

18 TUESDAY (108—257)

2. I S. Coffee Bar
London.

19 WEDNESDAY (109—256)

DONCASTER. BATHS HALL
4.00

4th Month APRIL, 1961 35
Apr. 17 to 23

20 THURSDAY (110—255)
P.A.Y.E. Week 3 begins

DARNALL PUBLIC HALL
8.00.

21 FRIDAY (111—254)
Queen Elizabeth II born, 1926

SWOLLOWNEST. WELFARE HALL

22 SATURDAY (112—253)
☽ First Quarter. s.r. 5.50, s.s. 8.8

DONCASTER BATHS HALL 9-30 - 10-30.
£12. 0. 0

23 SUNDAY (113—252)
3rd after Easter. S. George

BUTCHERS ARMS
NOON & NIGHT — THURNSCOE
£14. 0. 0.

A couple of pages from the band's 1961 diary including some regular gigs and an important venture to London

didn't portray the exciting new rock 'n' roll image at all, performing in dinner jackets, white shirts and bow-ties.

It was a completely different story with Jerry Lee Lewis who sauntered on stage, looked at the audience as though they were rubbish and showed a real rock 'n' roll attitude. I was also thrilled by Eddie Cochran and Gene Vincent when they appeared at The Gaumont.

My initial influences were provided by Vincent, Holly and Berry, whose name I adopted on stage. We featured all their hits when I began performing with The Cruisers in concert halls and pubs. We were never a band for the workingmen's clubs and I still have the group's diary for 1961 which shows we regularly worked six nights a week at places such as Swallownest Welfare Hall, Worksop's Monaco Ballroom, the upstairs dance hall at Frecheville Co-op and St James Hall - "Jimmy's" - in Chesterfield.

I had turned professional in 1960 when I was earning much more from performing

Have van will travel. I'm pictured here outside Club 60 at Shalesmoor, Sheffield

It is 1960 and I meet Cliff Richard, the biggest star around at that time, at Sheffield's Kenwood Park Hotel. Who would have guessed that we would both still be performing fifty years later?

on stage than I was taking home from my welding job. We would get between £10 and £20 per gig and most other people at that time were earning only £8-£10 for a full week's work. Even though the band was in demand and we had a full diary of engagements, people advised me against it, saying I would be foolish to risk everything. After all, a career in music couldn't possibly last, could it? I left work, became a professional performer and the headline in the *Sheffield Star* read "Now it's all music" but I kept my welding gear close at hand, just in case.

I did get the support of my family who had all helped out at some of our early gigs. Mum worked the cloakroom, dad looked after the money and somebody's friend helped Martin, my cousin, play records. Dad also advised me when we required our own transport, suggesting that having a band-owned communal van would cause problems. So I learned to drive, bought an old Bedford, fitted a roof-rack and had my name painted down the sides.

We began travelling to gigs at The Oasis in Manchester and The Cavern in Liverpool and as the fame of Dave Berry and The Cruisers began to spread, so did our repertoire. We introduced more rhythm and blues numbers including music by John Lee Hooker and Jimmy Reed and people came along to our gigs specifically to hear which new songs we were doing. They were curious to know where we had found our songs and who had recorded them. Even though we were so busy we were

Smile please... my first publicity picture

Developing my familiar 'man in black" image... with only the shoes to go!

conscientious too and always made time for rehearsals, renting out a room in Beighton a couple of mornings each week so we could keep our act fresh with new songs.

There were a few changes to the band's line-up, particularly on drums where we had four different performers inside three years. Alan also quit when he went off to study at Chelsea Art College and he was replaced by Roy Barber.

One thing which made Dave Berry and The Cruisers unusual was that we promoted many of our own gigs. If we were asked to travel further afield we would book other Sheffield bands to perform in our place at our regular venues, The Leeds Arms at Kiveton, Co-op

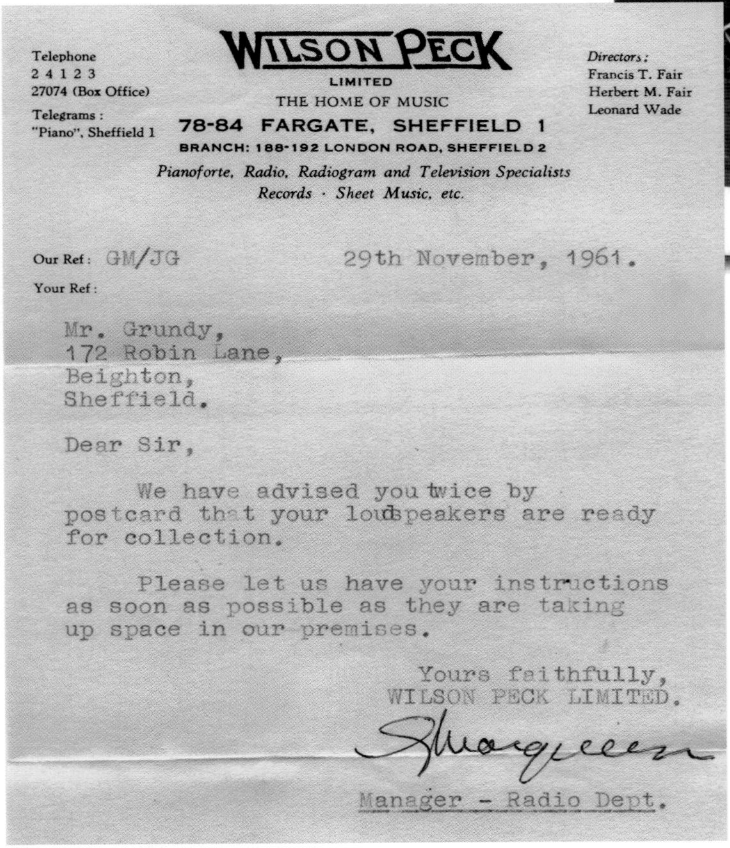

Telephone
24123
27074 (Box Office)
Telegrams :
"Piano", Sheffield 1

WILSON PECK
LIMITED
THE HOME OF MUSIC
78-84 FARGATE, SHEFFIELD 1
BRANCH: 188-192 LONDON ROAD, SHEFFIELD 2
Pianoforte, Radio, Radiogram and Television Specialists
Records · Sheet Music, etc.

Directors:
Francis T. Fair
Herbert M. Fair
Leonard Wade

Our Ref: GM/JG 29th November, 1961.
Your Ref:

Mr. Grundy,
172 Robin Lane,
Beighton,
Sheffield.

Dear Sir,

We have advised you twice by postcard that your loudspeakers are ready for collection.

Please let us have your instructions as soon as possible as they are taking up space in our premises.

Yours faithfully,
WILSON PECK LIMITED.

[signature]

Manager - Radio Dept.

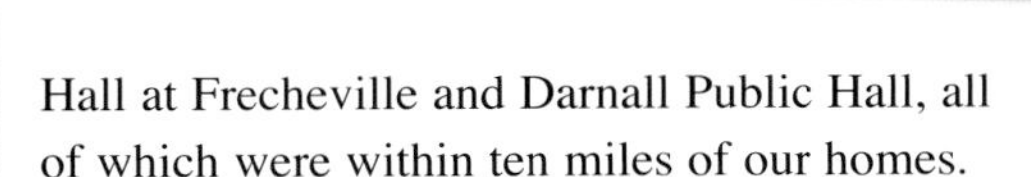

Hall at Frecheville and Darnall Public Hall, all of which were within ten miles of our homes.

The largest place we played in our early days was The Gaumont in Sheffield, a city centre picture house which staged regular Saturday morning music concerts for teenagers. There must have been six or seven hundred in the audience - a big step up from the numbers we had entertained at our usual halls and pubs.

I really must get around to picking up those loudspeakers one day

Readers of the Sheffield's Top Stars publication voted us their favourite local and national band for three successive years.

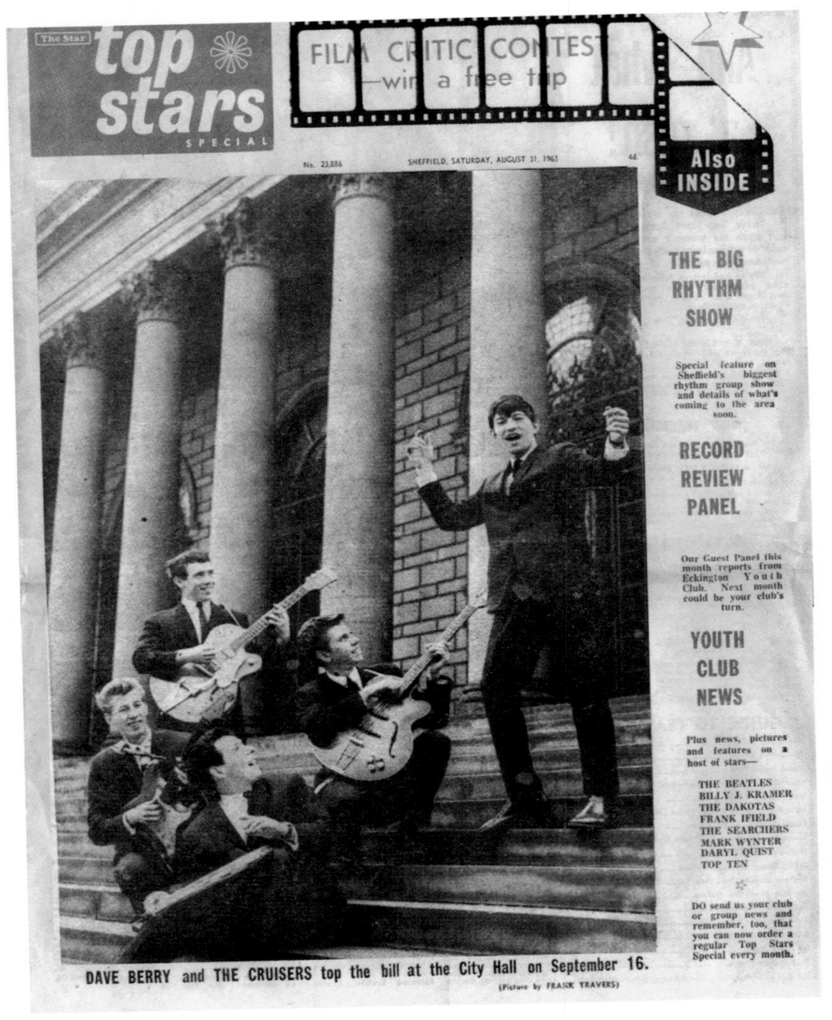

The Star
top stars
SPECIAL

FILM CRITIC CONTEST
—win a free trip

No. 23,886 SHEFFIELD, SATURDAY, AUGUST 31, 1963 4d.

DAVE BERRY and THE CRUISERS top the bill at the City Hall on September 16.

(Picture by FRANK TRAVERS)

Also INSIDE

THE BIG RHYTHM SHOW

Special feature on Sheffield's biggest rhythm group show and details of what's coming to the area soon.

RECORD REVIEW PANEL

Our Guest Panel this month reports from Eckington Youth Club. Next month could be your club's turn.

YOUTH CLUB NEWS

Plus news, pictures and features on a host of stars—

THE BEATLES
BILLY J. KRAMER
THE DAKOTAS
FRANK IFIELD
THE SEARCHERS
MARK WYNTER
DARYL QUIST
TOP TEN

DO send us your club or group news and remember, too, that you can now order a regular Top Stars Special every month.

It was always a gradual progression for us and soon we had even larger numbers watching us at grand ballroom venues. The Majestic at Hull had around 900 people in the audience when we appeared there.

Back in Sheffield, readers of the *Top Stars Special* newspaper voted us both the best local band and the top national band in 1961, 1962 and 1963 polls, even though at that stage we hadn't recorded a thing. Several other noted groups were on the scene in Sheffield in the early 1960s. Jimmy Crawford was the first local performer to have a big hit record with *I Love How You Love Me* and another popular act on the circuit was Johnny Tempest and The Cadillacs. There was another singer who was never really such a big attraction with the public, with many people regarding his performance as a little on the rough-and-ready side. Then known as Vance Arnold, he regularly played to just a handful of people with his band The Avengers at venues including The Penny Farthing and The Fleur de Lys at Totley on the outskirts of the city. Years later, when he enjoyed massive national and international fame under his real name, Joe Cocker, I was astonished at the number of people who claimed they had been there at the start of his career at all of those early gigs.

None of the up-and-coming bands were signed up with established agents in the entertainment world and people who represented us tended to be of a similar age to ourselves. Andrew Loog Oldham, who managed The Rolling Stones and was my publicist, was only 19 at the time.

Nowadays, celebrities are welcomed wherever they go but for rock 'n' roll performers in the early 1960s the hotel chains we are so familiar with today simply did not exist. We usually found ourselves staying in railway hotels which were large Victorian or Edwardian buildings. Most of the proprietors were not at all welcoming to young people in the music industry and they were certainly more comfortable entertaining businessmen. Some of the larger hotels absolutely despised musicians and the particular class of guests staying there all looked down on us. It was a strange situation because the businessmen

Dave thinks that Vance is great!

says CAROLE NEWTON

VANCE ARNOLD, who sings with the Avengers, is one of the most stylish and popular vocalists in Sheffield. His version of "Georgia" at the City Hall rhythm group show recently almost brought the house down.

Yet Vance himself is so shy that he refuses to talk about himself!

So just to fill in any omissions caused by Vance's reticence, a fan of his called into the office this week to put me in the picture (writes **Carole Newton).**

Who should it be but that talented Mr. Rhythm and Blues himself, Dave Berry — whose own first disc shot up eight places this week to occupy the 42 spot in the Top Fifty.

Feeling

"I think Vance and the Avengers are the greatest group in Sheffield today," raved Dave. "I go out of my way to see them whenever I can. They're probably one of the most original groups I've ever heard."

Dave has been watching Vance for a year now in pubs and clubs in the district, and feels he is one of the most under-rated singers in Sheffield.

"After hearing that boy sing 'Georgia' I hesitate to use it in my own act! He has a really good voice. He's no need to move around at all—all he needs to do is just stand there and sing and you're spellbound. He puts a tremendous amount of feeling into his work.

"His version of 'Ride On, Josephine,' just knocks me out. I'd really like to see this boy get the acclaim he deserves and as no one else seems to be doing anything about it, I thought I would."

Incidentally, Vance is 20, has been singing with the Avengers for two years, and works at the Gas Board. He has long curly brown hair and is quiet and shy—till he gets on stage.

He is a regular visitor to the Esquire Club.

And just for the record, Dave isn't the only Arnold fan in the district—everyone who saw him at the Sheffield Show is certain he won't be playing round the local clubs much longer.

I always rated Joe Cocker – alias Vance Arnold – and here is the proof from the September 1963 issue of Top Stars

The original Cruisers adopted the pseudonyms Johnny Dale, J.P. Nelson, Red Fleet and Wilson Shane

were there on their firms' expenses whereas I was paying for my own accommodation and also that of the band members.

The older generation didn't want to know us and those in the entertainment business could not accept the way our tours went out. We met a lot of opposition in theatres because all the big agents had been used to properly planned variety shows. The question was even asked: "Do you think show business will ever come back?"

Our performances were not structured at all and in many ways the people in the new bands coming through were just like those in their audiences. That is why rock and roll took off and has always been so successful, because fans can identify with the people up there entertaining them.

Hey Mr Tambourine Man... Letting rip with The Cruisers at Sheffield's Esquire Club, a venue later to become known as The Leadmill

On stage at another famous venue in the city, Club 60, in 1963

London Calling

LONDONERS GREET SHEFFIELD 'TEENAGERS SHOW WITH BOOS

Fighting Occurs as Stars from Beighton Do Their Act

AGENT WILL COME NORTH

THE Beighton rythm group "Dave Berry and The Cruisers" had a rough reception when they made their London debut at the Gaumont Theatre, Shepherd's Bush on Saturday—police had to be called after fighting broke out in the audience.

But the Beighton group were not the only ones to suffer. In fact the whole show — provided by 'teen-age rock 'n' roll stars who have made their mark on the stage at Sheffield Gaumont — took place before disturbances by young Londoners in the audience.

Dave Berry, better known in the ... area as Dave Grundy (21), ... Robin Lane, leader and ... vocalist of the ...

Our first venture to the capital was certainly one we would never forget, and it made good copy for the local newspapers

THEY called them the swinging sixties but the only things that were swinging when we made our London debut were people's fists.

Harry Murray, manager of the Sheffield Gaumont, had the excellent idea of travelling to the capital with a handful of local bands who regularly appeared on the bill at his Saturday morning Teenage Show. A couple of coach-loads of supporters went with us to the Gaumont Cinema in Shepherd's Bush.

It was March 1960 and, having been together for just six months or so, it was the biggest show to date for Dave Berry and The Cruisers. I celebrated by fitting out the band in new fawn-coloured jackets and Italian-style trousers, while I wore an all-white suit.

Unfortunately there was something of a reception party awaiting us and the compere and the first two acts - The Twin Cities and Mickey and Johnnie - were received with boos and catcalls and pelted with cigarette ends and empty matchboxes. The Londoners turned on our followers too and I was only halfway through our first number, *High School Confidential*, when everyone stood up and fighting broke out. Police arrived and there was a good old free-for-all. We carried on with our remaining three numbers but we were more or less playing to ourselves.

We did not return to the capital for more than a year, being invited to perform at the famous 2i's Coffee Bar venue where Cliff Richard - the biggest British music star of the time - had been discovered and where Tommy Steele had performed in the 1950s. It was very exciting for us and our fans were also thrilled.

The previous evening we had been on stage at The Monaco Ballroom in Worksop and immediately after our performance drove south to London through the night in the van - all four of us, our instruments and PA system. We arrived in Soho about 5am and almost froze to death sitting outside the venue waiting to be allowed in. I hated being in that van and the first thing I did when I made a bit of money was to make sure I travelled by car. Our

It is a serious business as I put pen to paper to sign a recording contract with Decca

following continued to grow and our fans from the early days remained loyal but they were anxious that we were not progressing as quickly as some of the other bands who had emerged on the scene. The Beatles first recorded in September 1962 and were suddenly the biggest thing around. Other groups we had been on a par with, such as The Hollies, Wayne Fontana and the Mindbenders and Freddie and the Dreamers, were all recording, had songs in the charts and were famous throughout the land.

Our fans were desperate to see us become successful nationally and we were testing their patience. Dave Berry and The Cruisers had been together for four years and everywhere we went people asked the same question: "Why aren't you recording like all the other bands?"

It was a particularly low point for us because we were not moving on; we were stuck. It was a time of monumental change in the music world and we feared that we would become such a disappointment to our fan base that they would give up on us and simply move on to follow other people.

We were being left by the wayside and became desperate to get something happening. The situation lasted for just a few months but at the time it seemed an eternity and was a major concern because we had put so much effort into everything.

Working with The Cruisers there had never been a great plan and I know it was the same with other bands. We were just the same as The Rolling Stones and The Beatles in thinking that if we got a few years work out of our music then that would be fine by us. We all knew that if music didn't work out for us we could always go back to normal jobs. Having trained as a welder, I was certainly no stranger to real work.

There was never a time when I considered giving up but, after seeing the Alexis Korner Blues Band two or three times in Sheffield, I did consider moving in a different direction by going to London to try to get gigs with jazzy blues types of bands.

Fortunately, in 1963 Mickie Most and Mike Smith from Decca Records travelled up from London to see us perform in Doncaster - at the swimming baths! Like many pools at the time, the water was covered with a false floor and the venue was quickly converted into a ballroom.

We were absolutely thrilled to sign a recording contract. We had achieved something for ourselves and also for our fans and things were moving again, even though I had to make a stand with Decca about keeping my stage name Dave Berry. With Chuck Berry and also Mike Berry on the scene it was suggested that I should become Dave Rand!

We went to Decca's West Hampstead studios in London and I don't think I have ever been as nervous and excited at the same time, turning up to our first recording session wearing a collar and tie.

Having signed us, I honestly don't think Decca really knew what to do with us and we went a long time looking for suitable material to record. The first track we released was a Chuck Berry song, *Memphis Tennessee*, which we had sung hundreds of times on stage. We had also performed it on the BBC radio programme, *Saturday Club*. On the record's B-side was *Tossin' and Turnin'* which had been a hit for Bobby Lewis in the States.

The Cruisers were top class musicians and were excellent on stage but for some reason it never really worked for us together in the studio. On our recording of *Memphis*, Decca chose to remove the original drumming by Pete Thornton and over-dub using a session musician. They also added their own piano and backing vocals. Our record company was intent on selling me as the front man and vocalist and the same thing happened with other bands, such as Peter Noone with his Herman's Hermits.

Mickie Most and Mike Smith didn't know the history of Dave Berry and The Cruisers and nothing was precious to them when they made decisions. They simply looked at us as a product they had to package and sell. The band had been with me for four years and now, just as we were on the verge of making the big time, they felt they were being discarded. They did a few things in the studio and continued to tour with me, but they were not on the chart records. It was unfortunate to see talented, loyal musicians being cast away in such a manner but that was the way things happened.

Once Decca explained that they wanted me to record with session musicians I was one hundred per cent behind the move. The people who I worked with knew all the music and arrangements, they were familiar with the studio surroundings and everything was done in a neat and tidy manner. They were young and talented and loved playing music. After doing their shift during the day they went out and played in bands at night. Big Jim Sullivan was a magnificent guitarist and Jimmy Page and John Paul Jones later went on to become half of Led Zeppelin. Recording with them was very clean and easy and they were open to suggestions too. It was the start of me having one band for the studio and another for the road, a situation I was very happy with.

My first appearance in the Top Twenty as recorded by the New Musical Express (left) and the Sheffield Star

NME TO[P 30]

(Wednesday, October 2, 1963)

Last Week	This Week	Title	Artist (Label)
2	1	DO YOU LOVE ME	Brian Poole and the Tremeloes (Decca)
1	2	SHE LOVES YOU	Beatles (Parlophone)
4	3	THEN HE KISSED ME	Crystals (London)
7	4	IF I HAD A HAMMER	Trini Lopez (Reprise)
5	5	I WANT TO STAY HERE	Steve Lawrence-Eydie Gorme (CBS)
10	6	SHINDIG	Shadows (Columbia)
13	7	BLUE BAYOU	Roy Orbison (London)
6	8	APPLEJACK	Jet Harris-Tony Meehan (Decca)
9	9	JUST LIKE EDDIE	Heinz (Decca)
3	10	IT'S ALL IN THE GAME	Cliff Richard (Columbia)
18	11	THE FIRST TIME	Adam Faith (Parlophone)
16	12	AIN'T GONNA KISS YA (EP)	Searchers (Pye)
8	13	BAD TO ME	Billy J. Kramer (Parlophone)
17	14	MEAN WOMAN BLUES	Roy Orbison (London)
11	15	I'LL NEVER GET OVER YOU	Johnny Kidd (HMV)
12	15	WISHING	Buddy Holly (Coral)
—	17	I	Shirley Bassey (Columbia)
21	18	HELLO MUDDUH, HELLO FADDUH	Allan Sherman (Warner Bros.)
26	19	SEARCHIN'	Hollies (Parlophone)
22	20	HELLO LITTLE GIRL	Fourmost (Parlophone)
14	21	YOU DON'T HAVE TO BE A BABY TO CRY	Caravelles (Decca-Ritz)
20	22	WHISPERING	Bachelors (Decca)
27	22	EVERYBODY	Tommy Roe (HMV)
24	24	STILL	Ken Dodd (Columbia)
30	25	DO YOU LOVE ME	Dave Clark Five (Columbia)
—	26	SOMEBODY ELSE'S GIRL	Billy Fury (Decca)
19	27	STILL	Karl Denver (Decca)
—	28	MY BOYFRIEND'S BACK	Angels (Mercury)
25	28	DANCE ON	Kathy Kirby (Decca)
—	30	MEMPHIS TENNESSEE	Dave Berry (Decca)

HE'S done it! "Memphis Tennessee" has soared into the Top Twenty—and Dave Berry makes local history by becoming the first Sheffield singer to make the Hit Parade with his first recording.

Congratulations, Dave. I'm sure all your fans will be as delighted as we are. I'm sure it will be the first of many.

And Dave has another reason to feel on top of the world. This month he begins his first nationwide tour, together with The Searchers and a solo Dusty Springfield.

Thrilled

"I'm thrilled to bits about my first major tour," Dave told **Carole Newton** when he returned from recording "Thank Your Lucky Stars" recently.

"I never expected the record to sell so well. I think my appearance on "Lucky Stars" boosted the sales tremendously.

"And I want to say a big 'Thank You' to all my fans in Sheffield—I couldn't have done it without them."

The tour commences on November 8, for ten days, and visits Sheffield's City Hall on the 16th. Also on the bill are Freddie and the Dreamers, who are among Dave's biggest fans when he plays in Manchester nightspots

Just as The Cruisers didn't work with me in the studio, neither did they accompany me much on TV shows. It suited me fine because appearing with a band would have restricted the way I was able to perform and be a showman. Being alone in front of the cameras gave me a blank canvas to work with.

My debut performance on TV was for Border TV in Carlisle where I sang both *Memphis* and *Tossin' and Turnin'*. I persuaded the show's producers to visit a local furniture shop and hire a bed for me to use in my performance. I didn't climb into it but I did sing standing next to the bedstead and mattress. On *Ready Steady Go* I began singing from the top of a spiral staircase, gradually winding my way down the steps throughout the whole of the song - something which looked great on the small screen but an act which would have been impossible with a backing band on stage with me.

Having released *Memphis*, my eyes were on the 'Hit Parade'. The weekly listings were compiled every Tuesday in order for them to be published in *Melody Maker* and *New Musical Express* at the weekend. My agent phoned me from Manchester to inform me Dave Berry and The Cruisers were a chart band at last but the biggest thrill came at the weekend when we were performing at Nelson Imperial Ballroom in Lancashire. The disc jockey there had the new Top 30 displayed in his box and it was so exciting to see *Memphis Tennessee* at number 28, just a week after being released.

The chart entry was also noted across the Atlantic and Chuck Berry's record company immediately responded by re-releasing his original recording of the song from 1958. Amazingly, two versions of the same song, recorded by singers with the same surname, were soon climbing up the chart; Chuck's rose to number five and mine achieved number 19, remaining in the charts for 13 weeks.

With Chuck in America, it was me who enjoyed most of the Press attention and I was invited to perform on TV shows including *Thank Your Lucky Stars*. My version of the song was also played on the *Juke Box Jury* programme hosted by David Jacobs.

Memphis Tennessee was a landmark song in my life but it also gave a kickstart to Chuck's own career and, on the back of the song's popularity, he came over here to tour. He told the pop magazine *Fab*: "That *Memphis* race was more exciting than the Kentucky Derby. What's more, my kids were on Dave's side and they told me not to leave England without his autograph. I hold him responsible for helping me get back in the charts, not only in England but in the States too."

Chuck's record company, Pye International, hosted a big reception in London for the American to meet radio producers and other influential people in the music business. I was invited to go along because of

MERSEYSIDE TOPS

Compiled with the assistance of Nems, Rushworths, Cranes Liverpool Radio Supplies, Allen Bros., and Top 50 Records.

1. SHE LOVES YOU – THE BEATLES
2. BAD TO ME – BILLY J. KRAMER
3. I WANT TO STAY HERE – STEVE and EDIE
4. IT'S ALL IN THE GAME – CLIFF RICHARD
5. I'M TELLING YOU NOW – FREDDIE AND THE DREAMERS
6. THEN HE KISSED ME – THE CRYSTALS
7. HELLO LITTLE GIRL – THE FOURMOST
8. I'LL NEVER GET OVER YOU – JOHNNY KIDD AND THE PIRATES
9. IT'S LOVE THAT REALLY COUNTS – THE MERSEYBEATS
10. WIPE OUT – THE SAFARIS
11. YOU DON'T HAVE TO BE A BABY TO CRY – THE CARAVELLES
12. COME ON – THE ROLLING STONES
13. SEARCHIN' – THE HOLLIES
14. IF I HAD A HAMMER – TRINI LOPEZ
15. MEMPHIS – DAVE BERRY
16. WHISPERING – THE BATCHELORS
17. TWIST AND SHOUT E.P. – THE BEATLES
18. APPLEJACK – JET HARRIS and TONY MEEHAN
19. SWEETS FOR MY SWEET – THE SEARCHERS

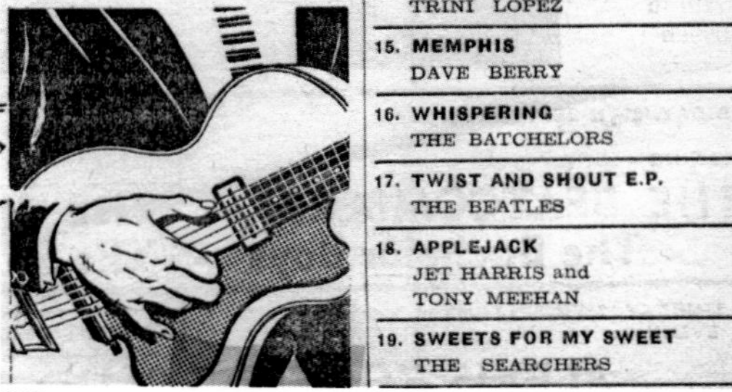

There were charts galore and in September 1963 I was thrilled to see my name in all of them

Taking steps to promote my recordings on TV's popular Ready Steady Go programme

A brace of Berrys. Chuck and I had versions of the same song in the chart at the same time

my connection - after all, I suppose I was the reason he was over here!

The general advice is never to meet up with your heroes in case they fail to match up to your impressions and expectations. Never was that adage truer than with Chuck Berry who was not a very friendly person at all. He was doing a show in Manchester and I went across the Pennines with my driver, Sam, to meet him. We booked into the same hotel and took him to the theatre at night. After the show Sam drove him back, then the following night we took him to Liverpool. There is usually a good camaraderie between musicians but there was none at all as far as Chuck was concerned. He didn't respond to any of our conversation... in fact he didn't say much at all. Keith Richard once said that Chuck was the only person ever to hit him after he had tried to start a conversation one evening. Keith and I clearly agreed that this was one American with a huge chip on his shoulder.

Chuck had been my big idol for several years so it was very disappointing for me to see the standard of his shows. I don't think he could have ever rehearsed with his band and the word was that the only qualification musicians needed to back him on stage was that they must have heard a Chuck Berry album. I just lost interest and stopped going to see him perform. Even though I had once enthusiastically tuned into a crackly radio station at 5.30am most mornings to try to catch his music, I wouldn't now cross the street to see him. Hero to zero, as they say.

CENTRAL
BEIGHTON

SUN., March 6th for 1 Day only
Steve Terrell
INVASION OF THE HELL CREATURES ⓧ
Also on the Stage at 7 p.m.
Straight from their London debut
DAVE BERRY and THE CRUISERS

MON March 7th For 3 Days
Gordon Scott, Anthony Quale
TARZAN'S GREATEST ADVENTURE Ⓤ
Technicolor

Now well-known nationally, we continued performing at local venues and this was a scary double-bill at the Beighton cinema

A GROUP with big - time success at their fingertips—Sheffield's Dave Berry and The Cruisers.

SHEFFIELD BLUES SINGER HITS THE HIT PARADE WITH HIS FIRST RECORD

POPULAR Sheffield rhythm-and-blues singer Dave Ber[ry] makes local history this week as his record "Memph[is] Tennessee" enters the Hit Parade at No. 20. This [is] the highest spot in the "pop" music charts ever reached [by] a local artiste with his first rec[ord]

'TEENAGE GIRLS [...] BEIGHTON'S NEW [...]

Success follows on big disc release

THE home of Beighton "pop" singer, Dave Berry, has been besieged by 'teenage girls this week wanting autographed photos following the release of his record "Memphis Tennessee" and his first television appearance.

Since its release on September 6th, the record has proved a hit and on Monday reached the British Top 50 . . . and was still moving swiftly up the charts.

Dave (22), told the "South Yorkshire Times" at his Robin Lane home this week that groups of schoolgirls had been calling at his home every day.

"I am out during the day and my mother has had to hand out photographs to them, I can't grumble because these are the people who are buying the record," said Dave.

His fan mail has also increased and Monday's postbag revealed a letter from a Sheffield girl bearing the names of 80 friends who all wanted autographed photos.

He said: "It is amazing what a record and television appearance can do. We have been doing this number for over two years and although

The set for Dave Berry's ABC-TV appearance.

DAVE HITS THE NATIONAL TOP TWENTY...

QUEUE FOR "POP" STAR

Three in harmony session

DAVE BERRY seen with Decca recording wizard MIKE SMITH. This week Dave's version of "Memphis Tennessee" makes a fair old jump.

SOME pretty strange things happen in the disc world. One is happening right now. Just look at the top thirty and you'll see a disc called "Memphis Tennessee" in. By two people. Both with the name 'Berry'. One is the fabulous R&B performer Chuck Berry, and the other is the unknown English lad Dave Berry. Or formerly unknown lad Davy Berry.

The mix-up came about when Dave, who hails from Yorkshire, was given a Decca recording contract, and decided to wax a song

SHEFFIELD pop idol Dave Berry and The Cruisers (l to right), Pete Thornton, Frank Miles, John Fleet and R Barber, pack their gear aboard ready for their first to of Britain.

DAVE BERRY GOES ON FIRST TOUR

HITTING the road—not to Memphis, just to Halifax—local singing idol Dave Berry on the first leg of 10-day nationwide tour.

Dave, who became a national name a couple of weeks back when his debut disc "Memphis Tennessee" shot into the Top Twenty, is dashing off to Halifax to join ex-Springfields vocalist Dusty Springfield for a quick rehearsal before the show there tonight.

His group, The Cruisers, will be backing Dusty for the duration of the tour, which visits Sheffield City Hall on Saturday, November 16.

Says Dave, who lives at Robin Lane, Beighton: "This doesn't mean we're deserting our Sheffield fans, although we're tickled pink about our first big tour, of course. We'll be playing in Sheffield another five times before Christmas."

My first record release, Memphis Tennessee, took me into the charts, onto people's TV screens and back into the newspapers

'Pop' star, riding high with record, takes to road

WITH his first record verging on the Top Twenty, Sheffield rhythm and blues singer, Dave Berry, and his group, The Cruisers, have been booked for a ten-day tour of the country next month.

Local fans will have a chance to see him. The tour includes a visit to Sheffield City Hall on Nov. 16.

They will appear on a "Top Pops" bill with Tommy Roe, Freddy and the Dreamers, Brian Poole and the Searchers. The tour also includes Halifax, Bolton, Liverpool, Cannock, Tunbridge Wells, Brighton, Kettering and Leicester.

Dave, of Robin-Lane, Beighton, Sheffield, said: "This will be our first national tour and we are all looking forward to it. I never expected our record to sell as well nationally as it is doing."

His record, "Memphis, Tennessee," is currently No. 25 in the charts. It is expected to rise even higher following his recent appearance on the ITV show, "Thank Your Lucky Stars."

The leader of the band usually gets all the attention, just as here at Shrewsbury Music Hall, and it led to unrest with the original Cruisers

A Few Changes

A new line-up for The Cruisers and I am now backed by, from left, Pete Cliffe, Frank White, John Riley and Alan Taylor

THERE was much bitterness when the original Cruisers and I eventually parted company towards the end of 1964 but that was what happened with lots of bands.

We had been together from the outset and they felt they had been very badly done to, mainly by being omitted from my studio recordings which were released by Dave Berry, not Dave Berry and The Cruisers. I had become very much the focal point of the group and they resented that.

There had been unrest for several months but it was never a personal thing. Perhaps they felt I should have held meetings with the record company insisting that we should use them in the studios, but I never did. Neither did I ever give them the credit they deserved. Recently, listening back to some of our original tracks I realise just how good the band really was.

At that time it was so difficult for us to appreciate the quality of the music we were making because we were on stage and there was no means of filming a performance and watching it back later, as musicians do nowadays. I have a tape of a

When news broke of my split from the original Cruisers, fans feared it would be the end of my career. However, I acted swiftly to recruit a new team of musicians and we are pictured here in the South Yorkshire Times

DAVE BERRY, Sheffield's Top Twenty pop singer, and his backing group The Cruisers are splitting up after being together for five years.

The split has come about because The Cruisers were dissatisfied with financial arrangements and felt they were being held back as a group without a full share of the limelight, says bass guitarist Johnny Fleet.

I was disgusted when I read that the Cruisers, Dave Berry's backing group were leaving him because they weren't getting enough money.

I heard that each of the group were getting at least £30 clear every week which isn't a bad wage.

Most groups are in the business because they like it and a lot of them play for virtually nothing.

Of course, they have got to live, but if the Cruisers don't think they can live on £30 they must have very expensive tastes.

It is a sad reflection if a group leave their singer at such a vital stage of his — and their — career purely for money.

I would have thought it a better proposition for them to wait and see if Dave Berry can follow up his chart number "The Crying Game".

I'm sure, after meeting Dave Berry, he wouldn't leave them without a good wage packet.

It just boils down to pure greed. I hope Dave Berry goes on and on to international stardom while the Cruisers stay at their present level — earning a mere £30 a week. Tony White, Widnes Road, Sheffield.

FRAMED BY THE TWIN NECKS OF A £400 GUITAR is Dave Berry with the new Cruisers. Left to right they are Frank White, Pete Cliffe, Johnny O'Reilly and Alan Taylor.

Dave has four new Cruisers for his backing group

LESS than a fortnight before his new disc is released, Beighton's Top 20 recording star, Dave Berry, has replaced all the members of his backing group, The Cruisers . . . and the newcomers are all locals.

The original Cruisers went on to become Joe Cocker's backing band. From left: Frank Miles, Roy Barber, Kenny Slade and John Fleet

performance we did at The Plaza at Handsworth in Sheffield in our early days, plus copies of some sessions we did for the BBC, and the sound really is special. Everyone was aware of the original Cruisers and knew how good they were; even The Beatles knew of our reputation from the road shows we were doing. Now, with the distance of time, I have been able to appreciate the excellence of what we did together.

When news of the split broke, it was suggested that it would mark the end of all our careers because the band had been a close unit for so long and we had created such an original sound. Supporters who had been with us for several years were very disappointed.

The Cruisers continued to work together, going on to become Joe Cocker's backing musicians, and I recruited Frank White and his band to replace them. Everyone knew of Frank's special guitar talent and I had wanted to work with him since I first saw him backing Jimmy Crawford. It was a privilege to have him as part of my band from 1964-66 and he accompanied me on tours with The Rolling Stones and also when I performed in Europe. Frank has always commanded the greatest respect from his fellow musicians and even now whenever I see legendary guitarists such as Jeff Beck or Jimmy Page they always ask about him. Frank joined my new-look band with drummer John Riley, Pete Cliffe on bass and my old friend Alan Taylor who had completed his studies at Chelsea Art College. They were the second generation of Cruisers to tour with me.

The band's line-up was seldom static and throughout the seventies and eighties the Cruisers' name disappeared completely when I chose to be backed by Sheffield musicians The Daizies, then Manchester-based Richard Kent Style who also performed with Paul Jones and Del Shannon. There was The John Verity Band, my old friend Frank White and his band, then the Birmingham-based Chris Lomas Band who played with me for three years. In 1980 I was supported by Bradford musicians and then a line-up from Macclesfield from 1982 through to 1989.

Nowadays The Cruisers comprise Brian Wood who has been with me for 20 years on bass and lap steel guitar, his nephew Jason Anthony Wood on lead guitar, John Firminger who has been a stalwart on drums for 12 years and guitarist Johnny Marchette who was just 17 when he joined the band five years ago. This is the most permanent band line-up I have ever had and adding more youth to our outlook is our sound engineer James Campbell, aged eighteen.

There is something particularly dramatic about black

Black Berry

ELVIS Presley said there are two great colours that leap out from any stage: pink and black. I've never gone for pink myself but I have always felt there is something particularly dramatic about black. I have worn dark clothing throughout most of my career and off stage I have a love for black and white photography; some of the greatest pictures ever taken have been black and white images.

Other performers have also been famous for their black stage clothing, including Roy Orbison and one of the greatest influences on my career and image, Johnny Cash. I first heard of him in the late 1950s and saw him live when he toured over here a few years later. He was doing a show in Birmingham and when The Cruisers and I discovered we would be passing close by during our own tour, I contacted the promoter and arranged for us to see him, later also taking in his show in Manchester.

You don't require a perfect voice to make a career in pop music; that's not what it is all about. When I first heard Johnny Cash he sang in a monotone which immediately appealed to me and that is the way I

Whatever the era and
whatever the song, black
has remained my colour
Dave
Berry

perform. We have completely different voices and although mine is not the best in the world, singing in a similar manner to Johnny just seemed to fit.

I have around 15 of Johnny's albums in my collection and the *Hurt* video he made is the most moving one I have ever seen in my life. He knew he was dying when he filmed it and it was so distressing that his family said they simply could not watch it. Johnny was an awesome entertainer and I continued going to see him until his final tour.

Inspecting my collection of Johnny Cash LPs with younger sister Julia

Gene Vincent, pub strippers and circus acts from Blackpool all played important roles as I formulated my own unique stage image. I had been impressed by Vincent's striking appearance in black leather and when I started out I used to try to be just like him, standing completely still as I sang.

Later, learning to take the microphone from its stand, I developed my act as something of a tease, beckoning the audience with slow-motion movements, turning away from them and letting the mike slide down my back. I'm sure all that came from me having seen strippers performing on the circuit while I was waiting to go on stage to sing.

One night in a tiny club in Sheffield it was so packed that no-one could move, least of all me with my big feet, and I had to perform. I couldn't just stand there and sing so I began acting about, hiding behind the collar of my coat, sinking my head behind it and holding the mike close to my mouth as I stood on the spot. The audience seemed to love it so I stuck with it. I did everything so slowly and my act grabbed the fans like a snake gets a rabbit.

I picked up valuable advice about my appearance from Blackpool circus performer Trixie Frankette and her husband, Arnold. I met them when I sang at the Picador Club which they owned, next door to the seaside town's Bloomfield Road football ground. They were friendly with many other circus acts who, when they came down from performing on top of Blackpool Tower, always looked very smart indeed. I learned from them how important it was to be well turned out at all times, maintaining an impressive image even when you were not performing. That has stuck with me throughout my life and even now if I know I am going somewhere where the public will be around, I try to look as reasonable as I can.

I believe men aged over thirty should be banned from wearing jeans and pony-tails should be ruled out for everyone. Once when I appeared with Jasper Carrott he asked the audience if they knew why they were called pony-tails. "Because if you lift them up at the back there is an arsehole underneath," he explained.

It is not always possible for me to look my best of course and one day I was out hiking across the tops of the Brecon Beacons - an exposed place where the SAS train - all wrapped up in my warmest hiking gear and wearing a hood to protect me from the elements. I passed a couple of other ramblers and was amazed when one of them said "It's Dave Berry, isn't it?" I wanted to know how on earth they had recognised me and she simply said, "It's those eyes."

DAVE
BERRY

Bands on the Fun

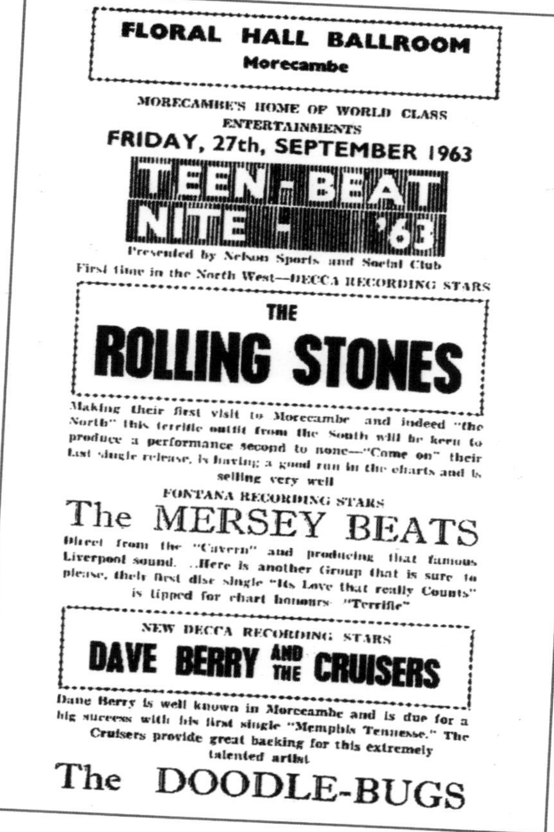

FLORAL HALL BALLROOM
Morecambe
MORECAMBE'S HOME OF WORLD CLASS ENTERTAINMENTS
FRIDAY, 27th, SEPTEMBER 1963
TEEN-BEAT NITE - '63
Presented by Nelson Sports and Social Club
First time in the North West—DECCA RECORDING STARS
THE
ROLLING STONES
Making their first visit to Morecambe and indeed "the North" this terrific outfit from the South will be keen to produce a performance second to none—"Come on" their last single release, is having a good run in the charts and is selling very well
FONTANA RECORDING STARS
The MERSEY BEATS
Direct from the "Cavern" and producing that famous Liverpool sound. ..Here is another Group that is sure to please, their first disc single "Its Love that really Counts" is tipped for chart honours "Terrific"
NEW DECCA RECORDING STARS
DAVE BERRY AND THE CRUISERS
Dave Berry is well known in Morecambe and is due for a big success with his first single "Memphis Tennesse." The Cruisers provide great backing for this extremely talented artist
The DOODLE-BUGS

ONE of my proudest possessions is a poster advertising a gig at Morecambe's Floral Hall in September 1963. It was the first time I appeared on the same bill as The Rolling Stones and we became good mates together when we went on tour the following year. Those were riotous times and you couldn't get in or out of the theatres because the kids were all going crazy. Both my band and the Stones had already had three or four years experience and we were confident performers having so much fun. We travelled alongside each other, stayed in the same hotels, drank together and went to clubs in various towns - well, those towns that had clubs.

I don't recall there ever being much rivalry between our bands; it was more a matter of us all getting along and having a laugh. The Hollies were sometimes a bit stand-offish and I remember a couple of them getting shirty one night after something had happened at a hotel, but generally everyone got along.

The Ronettes were the first black American female singers to tour Britain when they went on the road with my band and the Stones. When their legendary producer Phil Spector appeared a couple of times I remember Andrew Loog Oldham being completely in awe of the man who had invented "the wall of sound".

The image-conscious 'Man in Black' wearing a polo-necked sweater which even Val Doonican would have thought twice about

My first tour earlier that year had been with The Searchers, Dusty Springfield and Brian Poole and The Tremeloes but travelling around with the Stones was something else. We had a journalist with us, either from the *Daily Mail* or the *Express*, and whenever we were refused admission to a particular hotel or club because we were musicians, we could be certain that the story would be in the papers the following morning. The journalists were just like ourselves; they were young and starting out on their careers and if we were turned away from a hotel, so were they. These newspaper people were big fans of ours and they gave us amazing coverage in their publications.

There was plenty for them to write about when I travelled North of the Border with the Stones, Peter and Gordon, Freddie and the Dreamers and Millie. I had never imagined fans in Scotland would be as

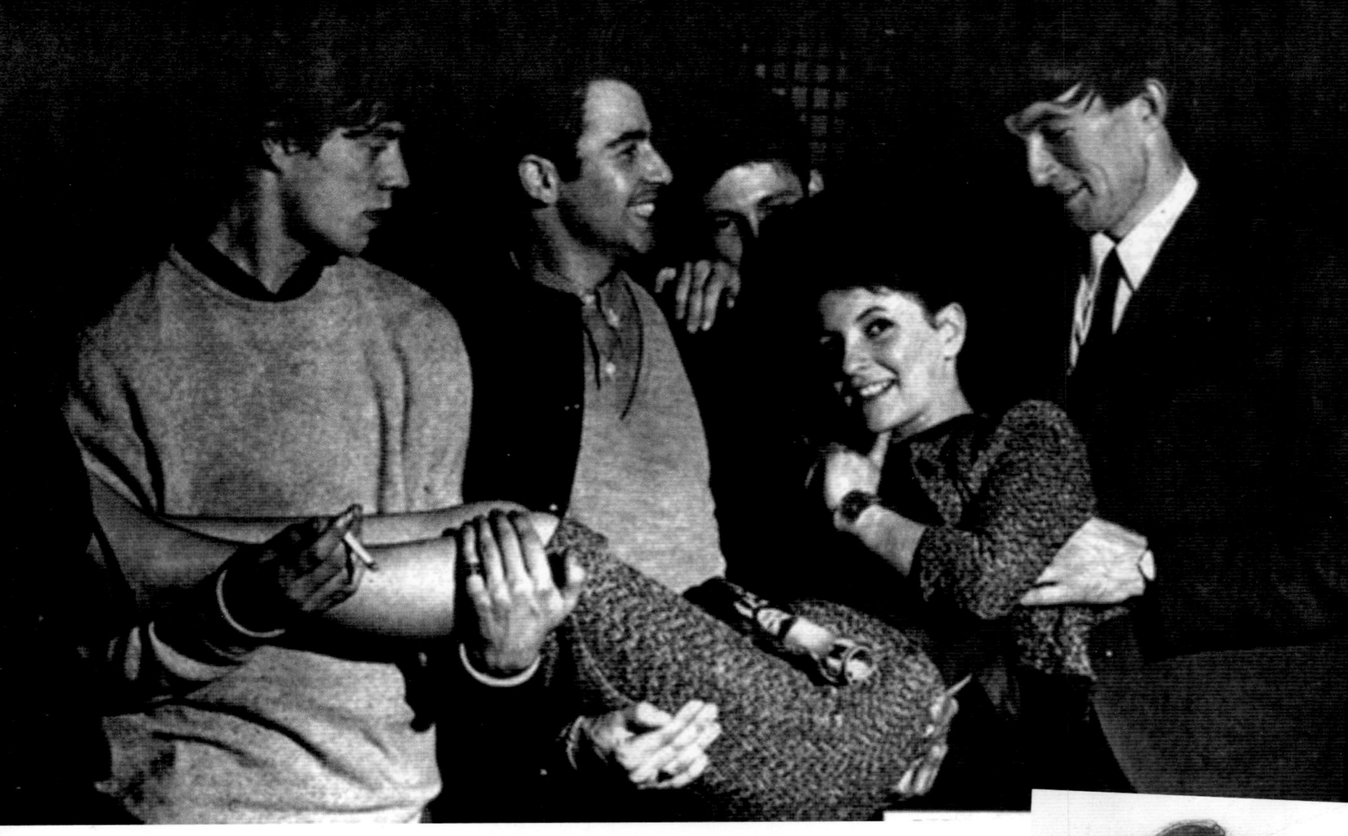

Party time at Decca and the recording company's Beryl Marsden gets a lift from me with the help of Mick Jagger (with cigarette) and other performers

enthusiastic as they were in England, but I was proved wrong on the first night of our tour. We opened at a dance hall in Hamilton where, in addition to the 2,500 people inside, a number of forged tickets meant there were at least another 1,000 fans locked out.

Almost 300 policemen and Red Cross members were on duty and they were needed too with rioting fans trying to break down a barrier and others fainting all over the place. I had never seen anything quite like it before; it was just like performing in a hospital. The dance was due to finish at midnight but it went on until 2.30am.

One particular incident which happened near to Romford in March 1965 was blown completely out of proportion, but it did wonders for the notoriety of the Stones. Travelling in a fleet of cars late at night, we pulled into a petrol station. Some of the band members asked if there was a toilet they could use but when they learned there wasn't one, they just relieved themselves outside. Someone called the police and Mick Jagger, Bill Wyman and Brian Jones were arrested and charged with insulting behaviour. Our touring journalist was on the spot and the story made huge headlines in the nationals the following day, prompting a nationwide outrage.

Several years later, a similar thing happened to me in Staffordshire after a show. It was about two-thirty in the morning and, desperate to find a toilet, I called into an all-night garage. I asked the girl behind the counter if there was a gents I could use. There wasn't, but a policewoman standing behind me who had called in to buy a bar of chocolate had heard our conversation. I walked around a corner into the dark, completely out of sight, and had just started to pee when the policewoman startled me. Having followed me and knowing how desperate I was, she advised me that I was committing an offence. I thought she was joking because there was no-one else around to offend but she was serious and told me that if I wanted to argue about it she would take me to the police station. I was furious until I realised the name of the town I was in.... Leek!

Although we were all thrilled about the exciting new music we were producing, we generally looked up to the previous generation of entertainers and it was an honour for me to tour with Billy Fury. For one thing, he taught me good manners. He was such a pleasant and polite person to work alongside and one evening I remember him knocking on my dressing room door, asking if he could possibly come in to use the bathroom. Anyone else would have simply barged in. I have always remembered that and even now I always try to be polite backstage and won't walk into anyone's dressing room unless I am invited in or I ask first.

I did shows with The Who and afterwards I would

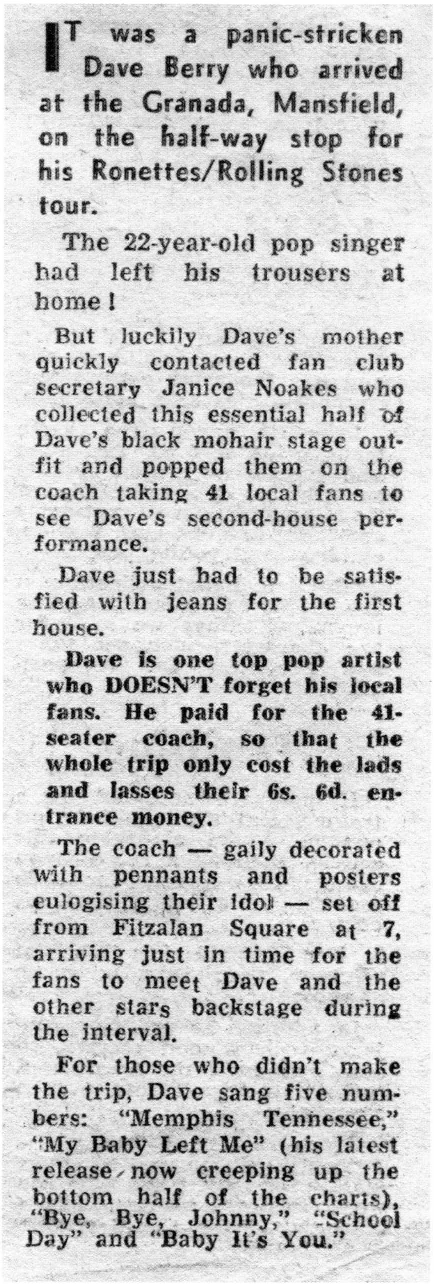

IT was a panic-stricken Dave Berry who arrived at the Granada, Mansfield, on the half-way stop for his Ronettes/Rolling Stones tour.

The 22-year-old pop singer had left his trousers at home!

But luckily Dave's mother quickly contacted fan club secretary Janice Noakes who collected this essential half of Dave's black mohair stage outfit and popped them on the coach taking 41 local fans to see Dave's second-house performance.

Dave just had to be satisfied with jeans for the first house.

Dave is one top pop artist who DOESN'T forget his local fans. He paid for the 41-seater coach, so that the whole trip only cost the lads and lasses their 6s. 6d. entrance money.

The coach — gaily decorated with pennants and posters eulogising their idol — set off from Fitzalan Square at 7, arriving just in time for the fans to meet Dave and the other stars backstage during the interval.

For those who didn't make the trip, Dave sang five numbers: "Memphis Tennessee," "My Baby Left Me" (his latest release, now creeping up the bottom half of the charts), "Bye, Bye, Johnny," "School Day" and "Baby It's You."

On tour with The Ronettes at Mansfield in 1964 (left) but minus my trousers (above)

It was suggested that I should try to have a stabilising influence on Peter Noone's young band, Herman's Hermits, but they were asking the wrong man

sit with Roger Daltrey and his colleagues in the hotel, relaxing with a few drinks. I never saw any of them throw TV sets through the hotel windows and whenever I read about their supposed exploits in the newspapers I knew to take everything with a pinch of salt.

In 1964 I toured with Peter Noone's young band, Herman's Hermits, and they were thrilled to be on the road for the first time. They were all enthusiastic teenagers and, although my band had only been touring for a year or so, we were definitely the more experienced outfit. We struck up a good friendship and had so many laughs. The hotels we stayed in all had cocktail bars and Peter and I would play a game inventing our own ridiculous drinks. It was hilarious and we had a riot together. Our agent, Danny Betesch, summoned me to his office in Manchester where he suggested I should try to have a stabilising influence on the young Herman's Hermits band members. I told him that as I was used to touring with the Stones and had lived in Hamburg's notorious Reeperbahn district, I was probably not in a position to be a stabilising figure for anyone!

I was lucky enough to tour with the fabulous Dusty Springfield four times and there were always so many parties going on. If it was the birthday of anyone remotely connected to our shows we would stage a party to celebrate. Another female singer I saw perform at a very tender age was Lulu. She would have been no older than sixteen when we appeared together in Glasgow and, surrounded by her mum, dad and brothers, she was so proud because her first record had just been released. Two years later we appeared on TV together in a live New Year *Ready Steady Go* show where we sang the Ray Charles song, *What I Say*.

On tour most musicians got to know each other really well and I met up with many other top performers in TV studios where we all did the same shows. I was on *Ready Steady Go* with The Pretty Things, The Troggs and Roy Orbison who struck me as being a pretty quiet guy.

When we were not touring or doing TV work, there was lots of other work in rock clubs, town halls and theatres. At Sunderland Mayfair I appeared with The Who and Lulu and I recently discovered an old poster advertising a show at The Futurist Theatre, Scarborough, featuring Dave Berry and The Cruisers alongside Wayne Fontana and Van Morrison's band at the time, Them.

Looking back, there were some strange combinations of performers out on the road in what were known as 'package' tours. One unlikely trio of acts featured Jimi Hendrix with Engelbert Humperdinck and Dave Dee, Dozy, Beaky, Mick and Titch!

It was always exciting meeting someone else from your profession, particularly when it was a performer whose work you admired. The Beatles were the biggest band of them all and although we were on the road at the same time, playing the same venues, I never got to meet them in the 1960s. I saw them perform when Peter Stringfellow put them on at The

HAROLD DAVISON & TITO BURNS PRESENT
DUSTY SPRINGFIELD
with the ECHOES
DUSTY'S SPECIAL GUESTS . . . .
DAVE BERRY ★ LOS BRAVOS ★ THE MINDBENDERS
Sept. 27 - 28
Except Sept. 27 - 28 Oct. 8
Sept. 27 - Oct. 3
BOZ & HIS GROUP
JEFFREY LENNER your Compere
DAVID & JONATHAN
Sept. 28
THE SETTLERS
EPISODE SIX
THE ALAN PRICE SET
London, Sept. 27 FINSBURY PARK ASTORIA 6.40 & 9.10
Bournemouth, Sept. 28 WINTER GARDENS 6.15 & 8.40
Cheltenham, Sept. 29 ODEON 6.15 & 8.45
Birmingham, Sept. 30 ODEON 6.45 & 9.00
Cardiff, Oct. 1 CAPITOL 6.00 & 8.30
Bristol, Oct. 2 COLSTON HALL 5.45 & 8.00
Manchester, Oct. 3 ODEON 6.15 & 8.45
Newcastle, Oct. 4 ODEON 6.15 & 8.45
Liverpool, Oct. 5 ODEON 6.35 & 8.50
Hanley, Oct. 6 GAUMONT 6.35 & 9.00
Sheffield, Oct. 7 GAUMONT 6.15 & 8.45
Leicester, Oct. 8 ODEON 6.00 & 8.30

It was always party time whenever I toured with the fabulous Dusty Springfield

Azena in Sheffield and later The Cruisers travelled to Doncaster - without me - to see them play at the Baths Hall, going backstage after the show to meet John, Paul, George and Ringo.

My sister Julia got much closer to The Beatles than I did when she went out with Paul's brother Mike - a member of The Scaffold - for a while and was invited to the family home. I met The Beatles' manager Brian Epstein at the Grande Gala Du Disque in Amsterdam where another Liverpudlian, Cilla Black, was also on the bill. It was suggested that I might tour with The Beatles on what turned out to be their final run of performances in the UK before they split up.

Pictured in a continental pop music magazine with Cilla Black. I met her in Amsterdam when it was suggested that I might tour with another popular Liverpool act of the time, The Beatles

It was to take me more than thirty years to finally meet up with Paul McCartney. Here we are on stage at a celebration of Buddy Holly music with Gary Glitter, Alan Clarke of The Hollies and Dave Dee

I loved The Beatles' music and still do and without any doubt they have been the finest songwriters of the past fifty years. Although it would have been prestigious to be on the same bill as them, I feared I would have been lost in all the attention they would receive. They were being whisked into venues through the back door, put on stage for 35 minutes in front of thousands of screaming girls and then marched away again. No-one in the audiences would have been going along to see me and my band and I thought it wouldn't be the best move for me at that stage of my career. Cliff Bennett and the Rebel Rousers eventually undertook the tour with The Beatles and when I spoke to Cliff afterwards he confirmed that the whole experience had been a complete waste of time for them, as it would have been for any other artist.

It was to take until 1995 until I met Paul McCartney when I and several other performers were invited to a private party at a restaurant in London's Leicester Square. Paul had recently bought Buddy Holly's back catalogue and a CD was released featuring a variety of singers performing Buddy's classic songs. I was on there with my version of *Heartbeat*. I spoke with Paul, not about music but about my sister's 1960s friendship with his brother!

When you have been on the road for almost 50 years most towns and cities can look the same and sometimes you would not know if you were in Inverness or Plymouth. Entertainers can have lots of time on their hands between performances and I have always considered it to be important to have interests other than my music. A long stint away from home can be a real killer unless you have something else to do other than go on stage in the evening. I have seen so many people whose routine begins with a trip to the pub at 11am, returning to the hotel to sleep through the afternoon and then arrive at the theatre at 6.30pm, six days a week. I am convinced that many problems for people in the entertainment business - and this probably applies to professional sports people too - stem from having to endure long hours with not a great deal to do.

If I was in one town for several days I had my own routine, starting off with a visit to the library where I would spend two or three hours reading up about the

DAVE WA

Wend

Boiled e

and fr

local area and its history. I would walk around the town and familiarise myself with the railway station and bus station and get a feel for the place - something that doesn't quite match up with the image of a pop performer.

If there was an antiques auction locally I would go along to view the items the day before, do my show at night and then return for the sale the following day. I remember doing this in Truro where I soon discovered that the staff running the sale had been along to see me on stage just the night before. The auctioneer did a double-take when I raised my hand to bid for a piece of furniture. He looked up to see the same face he had been staring at in the concert hall.

Once in Bristol I bought a rather attractive, large wardrobe at an auction and it didn't quite squeeze into the back of my Volvo. It was sticking out a little way and I fastened it in place with some rope. The Colston Hall venue offered no parking close to the stage door and there was only a small loading bay. I didn't want to leave my car and valuable new purchase in a public car park so I asked a couple of my fellow performers to give me a hand to unload it and carry it backstage where it would be safe. Goodness knows what fans turning up for the concert thought when they saw Dave Berry, Gerry Marsden and Mike d'Abo carrying a large Victorian wardrobe down the street and into the theatre.

Travelling around the country gave me an opportunity to drop in on some of my fans... and I was rewarded with a breakfast of boiled egg and fruit here in Maidstone

AT HOME IN MAIDSTONE

as breakfast with her favourite pop star

aidstone G.P.O. telephone oper- or, 19 - year - old 'endy Hall enter- ined her favourite op star to breakfast n Tuesday.

And while she served 22- ar-old singer Dave Berry th a boiled egg and fruit, endy's mother stood at e front door on the okout for fans who might sturb the unexpected itor to their council use home in Nottingham enue, Maidstone.

"I wouldn't like a Coro- tion Street episode to ppen here," said Mrs. anche Hall. "You know, ting kids trying to see pop star and all that."

This week, Dave Berry's est record, "The Crying me," jumped from 21 to . 10 in the national

DAVE, on tour, was staying at Wilson's theatrical boarding-house. He'd lodged there before, at the start of his career. He liked the proprietor and his daughter.
DAVE BERRY AND THE STRANGER
DAVE! IT'S HALF-PAST. TIME YOU WERE ON YOUR WAY TO THE THEATRE.
THANKS, LINDA. I WAS LISTENING TO AN OLD BILL HALEY LP. DIDN'T REALISE IT WAS SO LATE.
DAVE BERRY! WE'VE HAD LOTS OF SHOWBIZ PEOPLE STAYING HERE, BUT I'VE NEVER COME ACROSS ANYONE AS RELAXED AS YOU.
WANT TO SEE THE SHOW? I CAN GET YOU A COMPLIMENTARY IF YOU LIKE.
I'D HAVE LOVED TO. BUT DAD'S AWAY ON BUSINESS AND SOMEONE HAS TO LOOK AFTER THE PLACE.
Without seeming to rush, Dave managed to be out of the house in thirty seconds flat.
I'LL PUT A FLASK OF COFFEE IN DAVE'S ROOM.
Later that evening there was a ring at the door.
DOES DAVE BERRY STAY HERE? I WONDER IF I COULD SEE HIM. TELL HIM IT'S AN OLD FRIEND.
I'M SORRY. HE'S AT THE THEATRE JUST NOW. HE WON'T BE BACK FOR AN HOUR AT LEAST.
OH. DO YOU THINK I COULD WAIT FOR HIM IN HIS ROOM?
WE-ELL. IT'S NOT VERY USUAL...BUT YOU SAY YOU'RE A PAL OF HIS?
I'M GEOFF MURRAY. WE USED TO KNOW EACH OTHER IN HAMBURG.
OH, WAS THAT WHEN HE WAS AT THE STAR CLUB, THEN?
THAT'S RIGH. HE WENT LIKE A BOMB.

Part of the Union

WORK SHEET – Week commencing SAT: 23rd OCTOBER, 1965. ARTISTE: DAVE BERRY AND THE CRUISE
****

DATE	VENUE	MANAGEMENT/AGENT	FEE	Payment A-Cash B-Cheque	Playing Times	Arri- at
SAT. 23 OCT:	P.A.'S : BOLTON and OLDHAM. STUDENTS' UNION, LIVERPOOL UNIVERSITY, BEDFORD STREET NORTH, LIVERPOOL, 7.	Doug. Eaton: Social Secretary.	£100 £225	B.	1x50	6-
SUN. 24 OCT:	---					
MON. 25 OCT:	---					
TUE. 26 OCT:	"POP INN", Paris Studio, LONDON.	BBC				12-
WED. 27 OCT:	"DISCS A GOGO", Television Centre, Bath Road, BRISTOL.	T.W.W. Limited: Chris Mercer.				1-
THUR. 28 OCT:	EMPIRE BALLROOM, NEATH.	Roger Wright: King's Agency Ltd.	£200 Split	A.	1x50	7-
FRI. 29 OCT:	DAVE ONLY: "READY STEADY GO", Wembley Studios. LEYTON BATHS, LEYTON, LONDON.	Rediffusion Television Ltd. Roy Tempest Organisation Ltd.	£17.10 £150 against 50%	B.	6-08 to 7-0	9- a.m

PLEASE NOTE: If, for any reason whatsoever, you are unable to reach a venue at the time specified please telephone the office at Manchester CENtral 5423/4/5

A hectic week of work for Dave Berry and The Cruisers in October, 1965

MANY young people who enjoy big successes can also suffer an attitude problem; I certainly did. Musicians and singers are often referred to as being difficult or even impossible to deal with because they want everything to be absolutely right for them. I went through a stage when whatever I said, that was it, and second-best just would not do.

I insisted that the lighting should be great, the sound should be spot-on and everyone should turn up as and when I wanted them to, giving me no less than 100 per cent. When sometimes that was not possible I demanded to know why and, partly because of my ego, I simply wasn't prepared to listen to anyone else's views on anything. I was taking care of everyone so I expected total dedication in return and I wasn't very happy whenever that was not the case.

In the early days we were excited about doing one of our first BBC radio recordings in London at the Paris Studios. I was the only driver and I had arranged to pick up all the band members for the trip. However, when we arrived in Doncaster to collect our drummer, Pete Thornton, he simply was not there. We waited for a while but he never showed up so, with time against us, we drove to London without him. I had to put the drum track down myself, then add backing vocals, plus my own lead vocals.

Often when I was singing in Holland or Belgium, guitarist Frank White would travel with me and we would be supported by a band of continental musicians. We caught a regular late morning flight from Manchester to Amsterdam so at around 8am my

Opposite: If you are wondering what happened next, so am I. We will have to read next week's magazine to find out!

All present and correct for a gig at Bristol Corn Exchange

driver Sam and I would call at Frank's home at Pitsmoor in Sheffield to collect him. The building would be in darkness virtually every time with Frank still fast asleep in bed. I spent many hours waiting in cars outside Frank's home.

Comedy actress Sheila Fearn was my girlfriend for a while and she did not understand why I accepted such unprofessional behaviour from my band members, suggesting that I should simply sack them when they let me down. It stressed me out and made me uptight because I knew that if there was anything at all wrong with a gig, everyone would be blaming Dave Berry.

I have always been a union person with a good work ethic and was proud of the way I took care of my band members. In my welding days I had been a member of the Transport and General Workers' Union, then I joined the Musicians' Union. I have now been an Equity member for over 40 years and even though these days I never get asked for proof of membership, I am still happy to pay my fees.

When we set up the band I was organised right from the word "go". From talking to fellow musicians I know that I was the only leader of a band who paid redundancy money to people when I finished using them. My accountant paid their wages every week, after deducting their tax, and they were given Terms of Employment forms. They were paid a retainer each week and then a fee for every show we did. All their hotel bills were taken care of and I provided all their transport. These conditions were unheard of anywhere else in the business in the 1960s and some of the guys later told me that because of the redundancy pay they received they didn't need to do any other work for quite a while, so they just went to the pub or spent their time fishing.

Elsewhere, I saw some of my friends in the music business treated very badly indeed. Performers who had huge successes in selling vast numbers of records in the UK and the USA finished up penniless and no-one could tell them where all the money had gone to. They were players and not business people. While they were undertaking huge tours, selling millions of records and being told how successful they were, their agents and managers were the ones who were cashing in. Nowadays people can turn to financial advisers for help but they were not around in the 1960s. I learned pretty quickly to question everything but, by doing that, it added to my reputation for being "difficult".

Because my success was a gradual process over several years, I was as well placed as anyone to know how to deal with adulation from fans when we became famous nationally and then internationally. There were times, however, when I wasn't sure why people wanted to meet up and talk to me; it was difficult to determine whether they were genuinely interested in the songs I sang or if they just wanted to be associated with me because I was famous.

As our fan base grew ever larger, the scenes at some of our concerts were astonishing. I lost several bracelets to people reaching out and making a grab for me and on one occasion I finished a show wearing just one shoe. Such behaviour from young people - teenage girls mostly, of course - was a new phenomenon in the 1960s and it was frowned upon by the older generation.

Headlines were written about me in the national Press after I performed before Princess Margaret in a "Beat Show" at Liverpool's Club Centre 63 in October, 1965. Screaming girls grabbed hold of my right leg and

Opposite: All in an evening's work for me but The Daily Sketch reports on something of a novelty for Princess Margaret

MARGARET SEES A POP STAR MOBBED

Dave Berry keeps right on singing for the Princess (arrowed) as the girls grab his legs and begin to drag him off.

By SKETCHREPORTER

PRINCESS MARGARET watched last night as a group of girls in front of her at a youth club dragged a pop singer from a stage.

Television singer, Dave Berry had to pass the Princess's chair to get back on stage after being rescued by stewards.

The beat session at the Club Centre 63, in Liverpool, was already in full swing when the Princess arrived for her visit.

The club became hotter as the teenagers began to dance, and the Princess took off her velvet fur-trimmed jacket.

POP GROUPS

She heard four pop groups. They were supposed to play for five minutes each, but she asked them to play for 15 minutes longer.

The club warden, the Rev. David Woodhouse, aged 29, said: "She told us she was sorry she could not stay longer and that she had thoroughly enjoyed it."

Crowds who had waited in the rain to see the Princess arrive were still there when she left to fly back to London.

With her she took a specially cut record of four songs by two Merseyside groups.

The songs on the record are not yet released and the cutting of the disc caused problems for the organisers, who succeeded in getting the copy back to Liverpool only a few hours before the Princess arrived.

pulled me from the stage as the Princess looked on. Fortunately, her security men left her side to come to my rescue and the show was able to continue.

Although we had reached a pinnacle in our careers, suddenly the standard of our music was not of such great importance to those people who came to our shows. They screamed as loudly as they could and were determined to pull me from the stage and as no-one could have possibly heard the music clearly, it became secondary to everything else that was going on.

In addition, instead of playing the two forty-five minute spots we had been used to each evening, because we were now sharing bills with groups such as The Hollies, The Ronettes, The Kinks and The Rolling Stones, we were only required to perform for twenty minutes or so. That only allowed time for a couple of our hits, our latest song and perhaps three or four others. The format didn't allow us to show off our ability or our diversity at all.

There were no complaints at the time because it was a fantastic experience and I would never have missed it for the world. I fully realise that my huge popularity in the 1960s is the reason people still want to see me on stage half-a-century later but we were musicians who were proud to be in a "proper band". As a performer, I have found it far more rewarding in more recent years when people have come along purely to listen to me and the band entertain them.

Always happy to sign autographs for teenage fans... plus one of their mums

Opposite: Contemplating the loss of another pair of shoes

DAVE BERRY...
...A REAL GREAT GUY!

Rock'n'Roll Rhythm and Blues

DAVE BERRY and

The Cruisers

Dances, Cabaret, Clubs, Parties, Weddings, etc.

Apply:-
DAVE BERRY, 172 ROBIN LANE, BEIGHTON, SHEFFIELD

ESQUIRE
XMAS 1964
ALL NIGHTER
with
DAVE BERRY and THE CRUISERS
JOE COCKERS BIG BLUES
THE SCOTT WILLIAM COMBO
DAVE HAWLEY
From Midnight Saturday, 26th December, to 6 a.m.

We were available for dances, parties and weddings... plus a very special Christmas all-nighter at Sheffield's city centre Esquire venue which also featured Joe Cocker and Richard Hawley's father, Dave

Baron of Rhythm and Blues

Dave Berry and the Cruisers

172 Robin Lane Beighton
Telephone 3198

From Fun to Fear

ANDREW Loog Oldham was a great creator of stories and images and one of his publicity stunts with me was to convince everyone I was into Zen Buddhism. I had heard Christmas Humphreys, a very famous judge in the sixties, talking about Buddhists and also read an article on the subject, but that was as far as it went until Andrew tipped people off and soon all the nationals were ringing me, wanting to know about my new religion.

I had to act quickly so I found a book in the library and learned nine or ten standard facts about Buddhism in order to help me respond to any of their questions. Soon everyone picked up the papers to read headlines about me believing in reincarnation and wanting to come back as a snake, probably a black mamba. I am sure the journalists realised it was nothing more than a stunt but it was a good tale for their newspapers and they all used it.

My local reporter friend Bryan Longworth helped me achieve more publicity with another concocted story after Decca received several requests for photographs of me from people in the Soviet Union. There had been 15 or maybe 20 letters addressed to "Dave Berry, London", most likely posted by Russians who had seen my name in a magazine or newspaper article. We put the story out that I had a huge fan base over there, adding that because the borders were so tightly controlled I couldn't get any money from the massive record sales I was achieving behind the Iron Curtain. One morning I had to get up for a 6am radio interview about the situation on the *Today* programme and I was also on Yorkshire TV.

DAVE BERRY is a very sensible lad.

He makes a habit of taking a holiday every three months to keep himself really up to scratch—unlike a lot of the pop stars who let themselves get overworked and end up in hospital.

Next on the list of holiday places Dave wants to visit are India and Japan. The reason? Well, Dave, you see, is very interested in Buddhism and wants to visit certain shrines abroad.

He's been interested in the subject for about six months now, after seeing a favourite programme on TV.

And talking of favourites, we'd like to bet that Dave is somewhere at the top of YOUR list!

When it comes to stories about pop performers you should certainly not believe everything you read in the papers... and I should know

Again, the whole thing was a complete fabrication.

Working with the Press in this way was all good fun and other artists later did exactly the same kind of things to promote themselves. However, there was one occasion when I was desperate to try to keep my name out of the papers. In fact I feared for my life.

Mandy Rice-Davies rumours

By DAVID SHARPE

Pop singer Dave Berry last night scotched rumours that he is dating cabaret artist Mandy Rice-Davies.

"There is no truth in the story going the rounds that we are to be married," said the Sheffield pop star.

The rumours began when Dave and Mandy were reported to have been seen together in Sheffield two days ago.

Mandy was appearing at a Doncaster club. She was in Sheffield at the time, booked in at a city centre hotel. Dave was staying at his home at Beighton, near Sheffield. He visited Sheffield during the afternoon.

Last night, at his home, Dave said: "I do admit that I am going out with a girl who has been mistaken, on several occasions, for Mandy Rice-Davies. But I certainly wasn't with Mandy on Monday."

Mandy's "double," he said, was a girl living in the Sheffield area. She was in show business, said Dave.

"I don't want to tell you who she is, because I don't think it is important enough. Anyway, with her being in the business, I don't want to do her any harm."

Bank visit

Was there any serious romance between the two? "Oh no. In fact we are not really going steady. I just take her out occasionally when I am in Sheffield. I take out quite a lot of girls."

Mandy, who was appearing at a club near Driffield last night, said that she did visit a bank in High Street, Sheffield, an Monday afternoon. And Dave agreed that he was "in the area of the bank" at the same time.

"But we didn't meet," they both said last night.

Dave, whose record "Little Things" yesterday entered the Top Twenty charts, would not say whether he was with the girl "who looks like Mandy" at the time.

At first both Dave and denied ever having met each other.

Mandy said late last night: "I have heard of Dave Berry —I think he made a record. But if we were in the same place at the same time its was pursely a coincidence.

Fearful about the consequences of my dates with Mandy Rice-Davies (right) I attempt to deny everything in the Morning Telegraph newspaper

It was in 1964 and my girlfriend was a certain young lady called Mandy Rice-Davies. Together with Christine Keeler, she was tied up in the biggest political scandal of the decade, the notorious Profumo Affair, which involved government ministers, wild sex parties, Russian spies, nuclear secrets... the lot.

Mandy was controlled by a team of infamous London gangsters who put her out as a singer on the cabaret circuit, which was how we came to meet. I first saw her at Webbington Country Club, near Weston-Super-Mare, and later watched her in a show with Bob Monkhouse and The Seekers at Greasbrough Club in Rotherham. We went on seeing each other for several months. She warned me from the outset that no-one could ever know that we were such close friends, otherwise it would be dangerous for both of us.

We only ever met each other in hotels as we toured the country, never daring to be together in public and Mandy never came to my shows. But our secret somehow got out and the *Morning Telegraph* in Sheffield contacted me one evening to inform me I had been seen with Mandy Rice-Davies in both Birmingham and Newcastle. At first I denied everything but I was really scared so after a while I contacted the paper's night editor to tell him I could be in serious danger if the story was published. The London gangsters would be on to us if the story was followed up by the national press, as it surely would be.

The Sheffield paper went ahead and printed what they knew but, for once, the nationals somehow failed to pick it up so the mob controlling Mandy never found out about our secret relationship. But believe me, I had been genuinely scared for my life.

I met Mandy again many years later in the 1990s when she appeared in a play at the Pomegranate Theatre in Chesterfield, just a few miles from my home. We just spent the afternoon walking around the town, enjoying cups of coffee and chatting about people we knew.

Opposite: Long Distance Information... Pictured with a bevy of beauties in Rave magazine

DAVE BERRY

Honest it's...

ABC T.V

HE sneaks across the stage, making weird movements with his large hands. He says he's a bit mad and you can't persuade him otherwise. He meets you wearing jeans, enormous buckled shoes, and a black sweater, with a sock tied round his head. He is very tall, with dark eyes that are no more than two slits in a large, well-constructed face. He pounces on you like a gleeful falcon, and grins widely. He is Dave Berry.

"I'm very weird," he said, quite seriously. "I feel odd, I've always felt odd." I mentioned that he looked a bit that way with a sock tied round his head.

"It was to remind me to meet you," he explained. "Good idea, don't you think?"

Dave is one of the few stars in this country whose act brought him fame before his hit records. His first really big hit was 'The Crying Game', yet he was well-established as a popular entertainer long before that.

"I started my working life as a welder in a steel factory. I hated it. The routine would have crushed my spirit in the end. I don't think young people should settle down to one job in one place too early in life."

Dave thinks that lots of young people today are in jobs that they dislike, and are leading lives that don't satisfy them. He'd like to see them get away, as he did.

"I always knew that I'd get away some day. There was a road leading out of town towards better things and I knew that I was meant to walk down it."

Nowadays life is a ball for Dave. He goes to bed at seven in the morning and gets up at one in the afternoon. This suits him fine. If he has to be in another town the next day, he and his road manager drive through the night, and go to bed when they arrive. If they don't have to travel, they give parties in their hotel room, or listen to records all night.

"I like the night," Dave explained. "I'm really a night owl. I feel good in the dark. I like wearing black and feeling black and lonely."

He recently took a holiday by himself in Algeria.

"The only thing I didn't like about the holiday was not being recognised. I suppose I'm conceited. I like to see people nudging each other and saying 'Look—there's Dave Berry.' I feel good when fans come up and talk to me. When I got back to London Airport after a trip, a few fans asked for my autograph and I was really pleased."

Dave likes going away by himself because he often feels out of touch with people. "They talk and I feel an outsider. My thoughts race on and soon I'm miles away from the conversation. Most people talk about nothing anyway. They waste their lives doing just that."

Boys like Dave who are big stars, living in the glamorous world of show-business, have to face a future when the fans won't care about them any more. Will they be happy then? Will they mind when they arrive at an airport and nobody recognises them or cares that they are home safely?

"We'll adjust. It's all a state of mind. If I've retired from the business, it won't actually matter commercially whether people recognise me or not. I think that part of my liking to be recognised is commercial. I don't admit it at the time, but the more they recognise me, the more I know they'll buy my records, and put money in my pockets."

I find that a lot of our pop stars talk about money. They don't pretend to be in the business for the glory or the love of it—just the money. Dave saves his money because he wants to buy a business later on.

"I also want to have an old house—a converted stable perhaps—where I can store myself away among antiques and piles of cash."

He laughs when he says this, but he's half serious too. He is an unusual boy with above average intelligence.

"My stage act is just an expression of myself," he said. "I think an act is really important. I am very aware of myself on stage. I get my friends to watch me on monitors in TV studios, and they tell me where I've gone wrong. I like constructive criticism."

He likes talking about his hand movements. "I'm an exhibitionist," he said, grinning amiably. "Most people in show-business are. I know that I've got something to give an audience and I give it."

How does a weird, self-centred, exhibitionist who likes the dark, and lonely holidays, feel about girls?

Again he was honest.

"I've got a lot of girls all over the country. I feel it's good to have a girl in every town, so to speak. I like them all. I'm not unkind to them but being busy travelling and all that, I don't have a lot of time to spend with them. It's a question of arriving, saying 'Get your coat on. We're off,' and then giving them a goodbye kiss. I'm always in a hurry. The day is just not long enough."

About his career he said, "I want to make hit records all the time. Recording companies don't make records for fun but to bring in the money. Anyone who says he doesn't want to make a hit record must be mad.

"Trouble with me is that I hate waiting for them to climb the charts. I get really fed-up watching their progress every week."

Those girls in Dave's life have to live in a hurry too. He's always in a rush. He talks fast, straight and to the point. He is enormously tall, nice and rather sweet. After I'd left him, he dashed off to some small town to meet a girl, do a show, and maybe walk beside black water.

Yes, he's certainly different— he's certainly Dave Berry.

NEXT WEEK!

Look out for another fab, extra-special feature by Dawn James. It's about a fab, extra-special girl—a real 'twinkling' star. Guessed it? Yes, you're right, it's TWINKLE.

An interview with Rave magazine reporter Dawn James

Top Ten Triumph

FANTASTIC!!
DAVE
BERRY
Baby it's you
F11876 45rpm

Baby It's You saw me return to the Top 30 but my following release was the one to take me into the top ten

ASK any performer to tell you the story behind their most successful recording and they will generally reply that they were convinced from the moment they first heard it that it was going to top the charts and be a smash hit. It didn't quite happen that way with me.

My A&R man, Mike Smith, gave me a roughly-mixed acetate recording of a song called *The Crying Game* along with several other tracks to consider for our recording sesssions. I listened to it but wasn't that impressed, mainly because it was a slow ballad and it wasn't the sort of thing I thought I should be recording. I'd had a minor hit with *Memphis* and my follow-up recording *My Baby Left Me*, written by Arthur Crudup, was a storming track which reached the top 40. *Baby It's You* peaked at number 27 and that was a slower song but I still saw myself as a rhythm 'n' blues singer and believed I should have been releasing similar things to the Rolling Stones. Recording a tear-jerking ballad after several years of fighting to popularise obscure American songs would surely have been letting the side down.

Months later, I was in the Decca studio working on different tracks when Jimmy Page and Big Jim Sullivan asked me to have another listen to *The Crying Game* which had been written with me in mind by a former schoolteacher, air traffic controller and silk screen printer, Geoff Stephens. They both thought it was a really good song. It had been a matter of me not being prepared to even consider recording anything I didn't want to, but when I witnessed how these two superb musicians were happy to diversify, working with The Kinks one day, Rolf Harris the next and then Herman's Hermits, I realised I was being too stubborn.

But even when I listened to it once again and then recorded it, I knew it was completely out of character for me and I couldn't help wondering what all the people back in Sheffield would think when they heard it. I much preferred the record's B-side, *Don't Gimme No Lip Child.* However, it soon became evident that *The Crying Game* was not just any old ballad and Big Jim Sullivan's spectacular guitar sounds, created with the help of a new De-Armond volume pedal device, were picked up on from the outset. It reached number five in the charts in August 1964 and by doing TV shows like *Thank Your Lucky Stars*, *Ready Steady Go* and a newish programmme called *Top of the Pops*, I was now attracting a different audience.

I am immensely proud to have been the first to record *The Crying Game* and, on one side of the Channel at least, it is the song everyone associates with me and it remains the most popular one in my stage show. It went on to be covered by Boy George in 1992 as the theme to the Neil Jordan movie, *The Crying Game*. Produced by the Pet Shop Boys, it turned out to be his last major hit single, making the UK chart in 1992. The song has also been recorded by artists including Brenda Lee, The Associates, Barbara Dickson, Chris Spedding, Blue System and Freddie Starr. My own favourite, however, was Kylie Minogue's version where the imagery was so similar to my own presentation. It was a thrill to discover that Kylie had clearly listened so closely to my original recording.

Performers such as The Merseybeats, The Searchers and Billy J. Kramer cheerfully chalked up successive chart hits but their popularity peaked for just 18 months or so. Although my hits were intermittent, my heyday was spread over five years and for some unknown reason I ended up having one big chart hit every year. After *Memphis* in 1963 and *The Crying Game* the following year, 1965 saw me record *Little Things*, written by Bobby Goldsborough, which peaked at number five.

I was prolific in the Decca studios, recording a hundred or so tracks, but my chart entry in 1966 was one of my least-favourite songs; in fact I was rather embarrassed when it began climbing the charts. Just as I had initially not rated *The Crying Game*, I thought *Mama* was not my kind of song at all. Although it certainly was not my idea to release it as a single, the record company representatives had their feelers out and when they reported back that it was a strong song which people responded to, I gave them the benefit of the doubt. *Mama* took me back to number five and proved far more popular than I would ever have imagined but, once again, I much preferred the livelier B-side track, *Walk Walk, Talk Talk. Mama* certainly struck a chord with many people and nowadays, if for some reason I don't include it in one of my shows, I can guarantee that someone will demand to know why.

There was a follow-up song to *Mama* and Dick Rowe - the Decca chief renowned for being the man who turned down The

THE CRYING GAME

by Geoff Stephens

I know all there is to know about the crying game.
I've had my share of the crying game.
First there are kisses
Then there are sighs
And then before you know where you are
You're saying goodbye.

One day soon I'm gonna tell the moon—about the crying game
And if he knows—maybe he'll explain
Why there are heartaches
Why there are tears
And what to do to stop feeling blue
When love disappears.

Don't want no more of the crying game
Don't want no more of the crying game.

© Copyright 1964
Southern Music Publishing Co. Ltd.

DAVE BERRY Real name David Berry Grundy. Born on February 6th, 1943, at Woodhouse, Sheffield. He's tall, dark, blue-eyed and very handsome. And he's a HIT!

The song which most people associate with me and one which I never tire of performing

Beatles - did his best to convince me to release it. Called *Daddy*, it had the same backing track and the awful opening line was "Who's the one who tickled your toes when you were young?" I went as far as recording it but thankfully it never saw the light of day.

I continued being busy in the Decca studios and several albums were released. My management there had plenty of confidence in me, allowing me to record material in many different styles, reflecting my love of jazz, blues, rock and country.

Although I remained rather a popular live entertainer and was regularly invited to do TV work, I did not chalk up as many top ten chart hits as I should have done. Perhaps one of the reasons was that I was regarded more as a visual performer than a recording artist. Denny Betesch remarked that when an audience watches a particularly entertaining performance, sometimes the songs don't always register with them. Perhaps in some ways I was ahead of the game; I was grateful to everyone who bought my singles and albums but my act would have been far better suited to the era of pop videos, DVDs and all those music channels on satellite TV.

However, new technology has breathed new life into my old work and black and white footage of some of my TV performances has emerged on YouTube, attracting tens of thousands of "hits". When I saw some of the clips on my computer, including one of me singing *The Crying Game* with Frank White on guitar, I was as surprised as anyone because they had been recorded in the studio to be broadcast on American TV's *Shindig* show and I had never ever seen them.

The Crying Game lifted me into the Top Ten in the Autumn of 1964, seeing me rub shoulders with the top artists of the time

WESTERN SCENE

TOP TEN

1 (3) **YOU'VE REALLY GOT ME**
The Kinks
(Pye)

2 (1) **HAVE I THE RIGHT**
The Honeycombs
(Pye)

3 (—) **I'M IN TO SOMETHING GOOD**
Herman's Hermits

4 (10) **THE CRYING GAME**
Dave Berry
(Decca)

5 (2) **DO WAH DIDDY**
Manfred Mann
(H.M.V.)

6 (—) **AS TEARS GO BY**
Marianne Faithfull
(Decca)

7 (7) **I GET AROUND**
Beachboys
(Capitol)

8 (5) **A HARD DAY'S NIGHT**
The Beatles
(Parlophone)

9 (—) **FIVE BY FIVE E.P.**
Rolling Stones
(Decca)

10 (4) **I WON'T FORGET YOU**
Jim Reeves
(R.C.A.-Victor)

(Previous positions indicated in brackets)

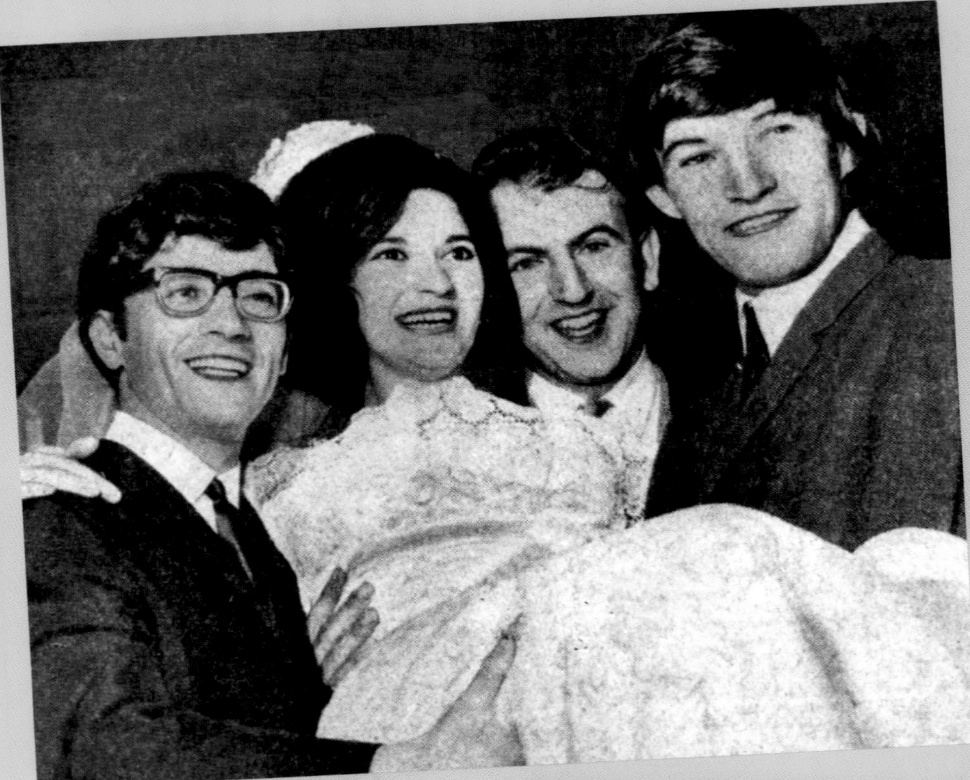

At the wedding of Danny Betesch, along with Freddie Garrity

Chilling out with Long John Baldry

1964 picture of Dave Berry and The Cruisers along with The Rolling Stones, Marty Wilde and The Wildcats, The Ronettes, The Swinging Blue Jeans and The Cheynes

Magazine poster of me with Neil Christian

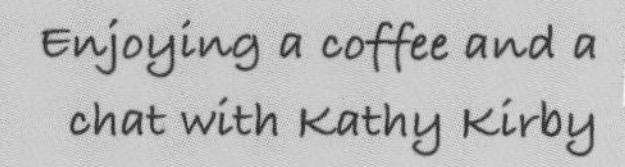

Enjoying a coffee and a chat with Kathy Kirby

Meeting singer/songwriters Alan Price and Georgie Fame

More coffee cups, this time with The Small Faces and Julie Rogers

The Strange Effect of Dave

by VICKY TRENT

One of the hottest prospects and certainly the guy I tip to be handling more hits than anyone in the future is Mr. Dave Berry. This guy has the biggest and strangest effect that any solo singer has had on the fans since Elvis or Cliff appeared on the scene and it seems amazing to me that Dave Berry should still be regarded as just another pop singer by many people. He has, to my mind, the best chance of anyone of being able to hit the charts and, to my mind again, of being one of the biggest and hottest actors and singers ever.

Yes, I did say actors. He really has something that is different. He has a face that is interesting but not specifically handsome. But it's the people with the "interesting" faces who get somewhere these days.

It's not the handsome gods like Fabian and Frankie Avalon who make the scene now. Take The Beatles and The Stones. They are good looking in a rough way but they strike more girls through the cupid clouds than do the swarthy Italian pop singers or indeed any of the French dark and handsome yodellers.

To be different is the big thing these days and it's certainly true that anyone or any person should be on the scene with something new before they get anywhere. Dave Berry is the singer who has stood out to my mind from all the new solo singers who have been launched over the past couple of years. He has a style and a stage act that is completely and utterly different from anyone else. He projects a fantastic TV image and he has made sure that he can make the scene with records that are distinctive and different enough to thrill his many fans. His latest record which has such a marvellous title and is certainly worth listening to, *This Strange Effect* deserves to make the charts at No. 1 wherever it is released.

For Dave Berry is a strange effect. He is a pop singer who is different. Different enough to make the scene whenever he wants to with new records. A different voice that, like Cliff's or Elvis's, you can recognise without having to be told that it is Dave's. To me he is the very tops in the scene and he is certainly someone who should make the charts with a very good No. 1 any time now. I hope that *This Strange Effect* is the record that does it.

T.V. fashion personality, Jackie Crier and one of The Gojos compete for Dave's famous lips. Dave Berry and Jackie Crier are appearing in "Thank Your Lucky Stars" Summer Spin.

From Pop Weekly magazine

Euro Adventures

EUROPE was a continent of extremes for me. On my first professional venture across the Channel I hated almost every moment and couldn't wait to return to Britain. But the continent also provided me with my biggest successes and I revelled in an adulation few artists ever experience.

The Beatles had recently returned from blazing a trail for British music in West Germany when The Cruisers and I were invited to head to Hamburg and Hanover in the Spring of 1962. This was our first major adventure as a band and when we learned that we were to play the same Top Ten Club venue as the "Fab Four" we were thrilled and excited.

I had only been abroad once before and to be told that we were going to be paid well for playing our music to enthusiastic German audiences for six weeks, and have accommodation provided, seemed like a major opportunity. However, the trip turned into a complete nightmare.

Travelling there by road, ferry and train, we had been contracted to play three forty-five minute spots per night but in reality the demand was for us to be on stage for about five hours every evening, working one hour on and one hour off until the next

Beighton 'beat' group to tour Germany this Summer

THE Beighton based "beat" group Dave Berry and the Cruisers, have landed their two biggest breaks in show business—a B.B.C. broadcast next Thursday and a three month tour of Germany this summer.

On Thursday, March 22nd, the Group will be playing in the live broadcast from Manchester of 'Teenagers Turn' at 5 p.m. and on May 1st they sail to Germany.

Dave, of Robin Lane, Beighton, told the 'South Yorkshire Times' this week that in Germany they will be playing in cabaret at such places at Frankfurt, Hamburg and Stuttgart.

"These are the breaks we have been waiting for and we hope to get into records through this in the near future," said Dave.

AND NORWAY ?

At the moment Dave and the Cruisers are playing at such places as Skegness and Morecambe in addition to local 'spots' at Frecheville Co-op. Hall. They have also played regularly at Darnall Public Hall and at Swallownest Miners' Welfare.

The other four members of the Group are Frank Miles, Woodhouse Lane, Beighton; Roy Barber, Foxwood Crescent, Intake; Kenny Slade of Chesterfield Road, Swallownest and Red Fleet, of Killamarsh.

We were initially thrilled to swap Skegness and Frecheville for Stuttgart and Frankfurt

morning. On Saturdays it was even worse, performing from 6pm until 6am in huge, cavernous places which served booze all night.

For a band which had previously been used to playing two forty-five minute spots each evening back in Britain, the demands being placed on us were exhausting. First, we decided to perform our repertoire a couple of times every evening but then we found ourselves playing other songs which we would otherwise never have dreamed of including, just to fill some of the time we were spending on stage.

Our so-called contract was to perform for six nights a week but we had to do Sunday shows too and when we finally returned, shattered, to our accommodation, the place was basic to say the least, with three beds in one room, four in another and a shared central kitchen.

The treatment was exactly the same for other bands too: Cliff Bennett and The Rebel Rousers, The Searchers and Dave Dee. So why did we stick it out? In truth, we didn't have any alternative as our passports had been taken from us when we arrived. Neither were we in a position to argue about our contracts because the management people sat in their office with a pair of Alsatian dogs and a gun beside them on the sofa.

The money we were on was an absolute pittance, particularly considering the long hours we worked, but one thing we did get out of the venture was an education. We met merchant seamen of many nationalities and, as as we were based next to Hamburg's famous red light quarter, we also got to know the local prostitutes who were employed at similar times to us. In fact, the band often worked longer hours and the girls would come into the clubs to see our show some time after 1am. We were just friendly with them and there was a tradition that if they had had a good night, they made sure that crates of beer were passed on to the stage for us.

Our German experience was absolutely awful and I was so desperate to return home that I spent half the money I had earned over the six weeks on a direct flight back to Manchester; I couldn't get back quick enough.

Looking back on those days, I'm sure everyone involved would say the experience was just a part of being a musician in the 1960s. I was in no rush to return but I did go back to Germany in the seventies and eighties when I enjoyed playing for enthusiastic fans at large festivals.

The exceptional successes I enjoyed in Holland and Belgium could quite easily never have happened. When my agent Danny Betesch invited me to travel with other Decca artists to Knokke in Belgium for an annual international song festival in May, 1965, it was really no big deal for me. In fact, if I'd had a prior booking with The Cruisers for that particular Saturday I wouldn't have even considered it.

However, I went over there with other performers including Adrienne Posta - a singer who later became better known as an actress - and jazz singer Joy Marshall. The event was a kind of mini Eurovision Song Contest and acts from Holland, Belgium, Germany and France also took part. It was an

Sheffield blues singer makes hit in Germany

SHEFFIELD'S popular rhythm and blues singer, Dave Berry, is currently completing a successful engagement in Germany.

With his instrumental group, The Cruisers, he has been appearing for the last three weeks at the Top Ten Club in Hamburg, where he has been given a great reception.

Already, a contract has been signed for a return visit in the very near future.

"ALWAYS PACKED"

"It has been a great experience," says Dave, who lives at Beighton. "Sunday shows start at 4 p.m. and last until 4 a.m. the following morning. The place is always packed from opening to close."

"Admission is cheap, but soft drinks are expensive," Dave added.

The 22-year-old, tall, dark-haired singer, who has a tremendous following in Sheffield and district, will be flying into Manchester next Monday on his way home.

Relieved to be on our way home, we put something of a gloss on our German experience when interviewed for the Sheffield Star

"HE'S immoral!"

That was the verdict of the German judges on Dave Berry last week at the European Singing Cup Contest held at Knokke-Le Zoute in Belgium. That wasn't all they said.

"He's a bad influence on the German people. He can't sing. He's sick!" At this point tempers frayed to breaking point. British judge Alan Freeman stepped in.

"Listen. The greatest entertainer in the world is a German. But she can't sing a note. Her name is Marlene Deitrich," he pointed out.

Norman Jopling reports on the Knokke-Le Zoute Contest . . .

The Germans were crushed. But it didn't stop them from marking Dave down. They gave him two out of ten. The rest of the judges gave him nine.

Just one of the incidents at Knokke, where everything opens peacefully and ends with a third world war in sight. We didn't win, although we had the best team. Really. Even the other teams and the foreign journalists thought so. Unfortunately the judges didn't.

During the week of the contest some interesting things happened. Like when Dave was doing cabaret, and singing "Can I Get It From You," making mock amorous advances to a pretty coloured lady in the audience "I love you baby," she yelled.

Dave was amazed when he found out it was **Dionne Warwick**. "She looks different" he complained.

My 'immoral' performance at Knokke won me the coveted Press Prize and it was lift-off time for my European career

established televised festival held in the large casino in Knokke and everyone except me wore formal evening suits and dickie-bows.

From the outset I decided that I would do my usual Dave Berry performance, so I simply treated it as just another gig. Backed by a large orchestra, I sang *This Strange Effect* - written for me by Ray Davies of The Kinks - and did my whole strange stage repertoire, hiding behind my hands and then slowly picking something off the floor. Much to my surprise, the audience took to it straight away... even though some of the international judges labelled me as being immoral and a danger to teenagers because I was not wearing evening dress.

The Decca team didn't win a thing but my performance landed the prestigious Press Prize, voted for by journalists from throughout Europe. That was a very special achievement indeed and it provided the springboard for an amazing sequence of successes for me. Within a couple of months I had five records in the Dutch charts and other big successes in Belgium and further afield.

I was aware that audiences in Holland and Belgium saw the humorous side of my stage performance and went for it one hundred per cent. They smiled when they saw me and I was delighted because I had always intended my stage show to be a little bit tongue-in-cheek. Strangely, I was always taken more seriously back home in Britain

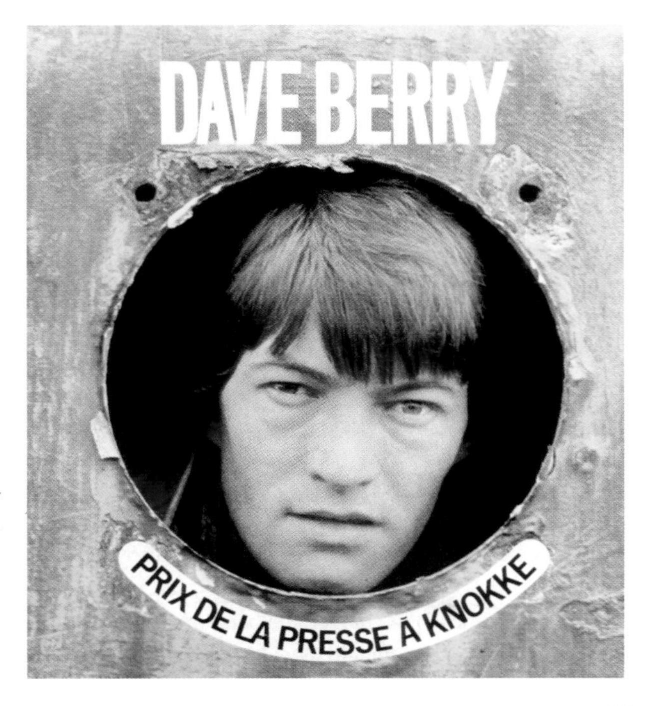

Berry heads for Dutch gold disc

DAVE BERRY'S "Strange Effect" is at No. 1 in the Dutch charts for the fourth successive week, and is rapidly approaching the hundred-thousand in sales, necessary to qualify for Netherland's Gold Disc.

He is again to visit Holland at the end of the month to play concerts at the Europe Hall, Calkamburg (November 26), Kuil Hall, Hapart (27), and the Prince Bernhard Hall, Zuibraen (28).

Five major TV dates have already been arranged as part of a U.S. promotional tour planned for December for Dave, but his agent Danny Bettesh is now awaiting an immigration permit.

This Strange Effect became the best-selling record of all time in Holland and Amsterdam's dockworkers donned their smartest overalls to see me receive a Gold Disc

Potige dokwerkers en gillende tieners

DAVE BERRY: EEN GOUDEN PLAAT N.D.S.M.: . . . GLASSCHERVEN . . .

De horde mag de hekken binnen ...... „een graantje meepikken" ......

Ongebruikelijke plechtigheid...

DE Engelse zanger Dave Berry heeft gisteren een gouden plaat gekregen voor „Strange effect", de Nederlandse Dok- en Scheepsbouw Maatschappij een hoop glasscherven. In een gigantisch en door de organisatoren niet bedoeld tumult heeft de NDSM gistermiddag bezoek gehad van Dave Berry. Wat aanvankelijk als een keurige, zij het enigsins ongebruikelijke plechtigheid leek te verlopen, ontaardde binnen het kwartier in een gejoel en een gedrang, waaruit Dave Berry slechts kon ontsnappen door onder allerlei tafeltjes door naar een buitendeur te koersen. Zijn pet, in Athene gekocht, verdween in de massa van honderden joelende dokwerkers en gillende tieners.

Het begon zo keurig met een gestencilde uitnodiging (gedateerd 15 december) van de platenmaatschappij Phonogram, waarin onder meer dit stond: „Door vriendelijke medewerking van de directie van de Nederlandse Dok- en Scheepsbouw Maatschappij in Amsterdam-Noord zal deze uitreiking op 22 december kunnen plaatsvinden in de lasloods, waar 125 lassers bezig zijn aan bouwnummer 500, de twaalf meter hoge, negentig ton wegende achter-

buiten de werfhekken (bewaakt door vier agenten te paard) „ook wel een graantje mochten meepikken". Dus werd Berry van de lasloods naar de bedrijfskantine vergezeld door een horde van zeker vijfhonderd tieners, aangevuld door personeel van de NDSM. In de kantine was een klein deel afgeschermd met hekken, die binnen de minuut bezweken onder de druk van de fans. Geen spreker kwam aan het woord, helemaal niet meer toen Berry — op het buffet staande —

Dokwerkers van de NDSM . . . snipperen voor Berry . . .

van een ruzie tussen een stel fans over de verdeling van Berry's petje. De NDSM heeft iets geleerd en Berry heeft het beloofde boek niet gekregen.

KRO's VERJAARDAG Rob de Nijs en

where people seemed to concentrate on the sinister side of my image.

Knokke was a major turning point in my career and *This Strange Effect* was soon at number one in the Belgian and Dutch charts. The song perfectly suited my stage act. It remained in the Top 40 for 35 weeks and I received a gold disc for 100,000 sales of the record - not bad at all for a country where the total population was about the same as that of London. I was told that 100,000 record sales in Holland was equivalent to a million sales in Britain.

When most record companies hand over Gold Discs to their most valued performers, they usually do so at a glamorous and elaborate ceremony. When Decca recognised my achievement, the presentation took place in an Amsterdam shipyard with me perched on scaffolding alongside a half-built ship. Actually, they made quite a big deal of it and the thinking behind the rather odd choice of location was because of my previous job as a welder. The workers there loved it and the presentation was given massive coverage in the newspapers.

My continental successes led to me being booked to appear on the big annual music show in Holland, the Grande Gala du Disque, staged at the Ria Centre in Amsterdam. Other performers included Diana Ross and The Supremes, The Everly Brothers, The Crickets, Cilla Black and top singers from France, Canada and elsewhere. It was another huge success for me and I thought the Dutch people were wonderful, putting so many of my records into their chart and then inviting me to play at their major music event of the year.

And it didn't stop there. I appeared on many Dutch TV shows and even

Nederlandse Hitparade december 1965

1. This Strange Effect - Dave Berry
2. Get off of my Cloud - The Rolling Stones
3. Sophietje - Johnny Lion
4. Here it comes again - The Fortunes
5. I'm gonna take you there - Daye Berry
6. Als ik de golven aan het strand zie - Ria Valk
7. You've got your Troubles - The Fortunes
8. Elke dag denk ik aan zondag - Willeke Alberti
9. Don't let the Stars... - Canadian Sweethaerts
10. Can I get it from you - Dave Berry
11. Capri c'est fini - Hervé Villard
12. Sittin' all alone - The Pretty Things
13. Een meisje van zestien - Boudewijn de Groot
14. A walk in the Black Forrest Horst Jankowski
15. Ride Away - Roy Orbison
16. What's new Pussycat - Tom Jones
17. Little Things - Dave Berry
18. Englands Swings - Roger Miller
19. It's good news Week - Hedgehoppers Anonymous
20. Wasted Words - The Motions.

Zanger

1. Cliff Richard	37.9 %
2. Donovan	15.1 %
3. Dave Berry	11.3 %
4. Elvis Presley	9.6 %
5. Bob Dylan	9.3 %
6. Adamo	9 %
7. Roy Orbison	4.1 %
8. Mick Jagger	1.9 %
9. Tom Jones	1 %
10. Barry Mc. Quire	0.8 %

I thought the Dutch music fans were wonderful for ensuring so many of my records entered their charts and in a continental poll of singers I was voted more popular than Elvis Presley, Mick Jagger and Tom Jones

NANCY C LEWIS LIMITED
73 WELLS STREET LONDON W1 LANgham 8761
MUSeum 0692/3

Londen, 27 januari 1966

Mijne Heren,

Op de hierbij ingesloten foto ziet U mij duiven vangen op Trafalgar Square in Londen. Op een van die vele druilerige Engelse zondagochtenden heb ik er een aantal gevangen en mee naar Sheffield genomen.

Op zaterdag 5 februari as. wil ik deze duiven om precies 12 uur 's middags weer loslaten op de Dam te Amsterdam.

Ik wil deze duiven aanbieden aan de zeer vele Nederlandse tieners en ouderen die mijn platen gekocht hebben (van "This strange effect" inmiddels reeds meer dan 160.000!). Daarom een koppel duiven voor Amsterdam - we hebben er in Londen nog genoeg over.

Behalve de duiven breng ik ook mijn orkest The Cruisers mee, want op 5 en 6 februari geven we een aantal concerten in Nederland. Die tweede datum is een dubbele feestdag voor mij, omdat ik op 6 februari 24 jaar hoop te worden. Ik vind het overigens bijzonder leuk om deze feestdag in Nederland te vieren!

Hopelijk kunt U in Uw blad een plaatsje voor de foto inruimen en zelf op 5 februari tijdig het bed verlaten.

Vr. groeten,

Dave Berry

A letter of invitation to my Dutch fans to join me in Amsterdam at the release of pigeons I had supposedly caught in London's Trafalgar Square

hosted my own programme where my guests included Tom Jones and The Fortunes.

The reaction from young Dutch fans was truly amazing and things reached an astonishing climax when a personal appearance was arranged in Amsterdam's Museum Square. The stunt was that I had brought along a basket of pigeons from London's Trafalgar Square to release in Amsterdam as a symbol of friendship. In truth, I would never have been allowed to take pigeons across the Channel, so they were Dutch birds.

I was appearing with The Cruisers at Toni Boltini's Circus that week and it was arranged for me to release the pigeons from a lion's cage in the centre of the square. But thousands of people were there, all wanting to see me, and all hell broke loose. I got into the cage for a brief moment but then, with people being crushed by police on horses, I was told that for everyone's safety I had to leave. Police and security men rushed me back to my hotel where I relaxed with a cup of coffee, oblivious to everything that was kicking off in the city centre. I had not realised the extent of the turmoil and was astonished later that evening when I watched the amazing riot scenes on a Dutch TV news programme. The event was also screened by *Pathe News* and, as a reminder, I have a DVD recording of the black and white film footage.

I reach the lion's cage in the centre of Amsterdam and sign a few autographs before being whisked back to my hotel as a safety measure

Dave niet in de leeuwenkooi

Baldadige tieners in Amsterdam

Enige duizenden tieners moesten zaterdagmiddag na vergeefs wachten op hun idool Dave Berry door politie van het Museumplein „geveegd" worden. Zij waren daar samengedromd om de Engelse tienerzanger een koppel duiven te zien lossen afkomstig van het Londense Trafalgar Square. Dit bedoeld als een „geschenk" aan de Nederlandse fans. Van de „happening" is echter niet veel terecht gekomen. In een leeuwenkooi zou Dave vóór komen rijden. Toen Dave Berry echter bij de in de Paulus Potterstraat geparkeerde leewenkooi van circus Boltini aankwam, was het voor hem al niet meer mogelijk er in te komen en te blijven. Grijpgrage handen demonteerden de kooi in een ommezien, zodat het voor de zanger gevaarlijk werd. Op slinkse wijze werd de kostbare Dave door zijn lijfwachten, de heer Boltini en enige heren van zijn platenmaatschappij „afgevoerd". De wachtende menigte begon toen onrustig te worden, teleurgesteld omdat hun idool niet aan de gestelde verwachtingen had voldaan. Uit baldadigheid vielen zij automobilisten lastig, gooiden stenen en deukten autodaken door erop te gaan staan. Motoragenten en bereden politie moesten een einde aan de wanorde maken, hetgeen nog geruime tijd in beslag nam. Dave voldeed wel aan zijn verplichtingen in Soesterberg, waar met zijn optreden min of meer officieel de permanente circusresidentie van Boltini als beatcentrum werd geopend. In de middag en 's avonds kreeg Dave de kans met zijn optreden en grapjes de tieners tot gillen te brengen. Vooral 's avonds was de belangstelling, ondanks de gepeperde prijzen, groot. Het legertje beschermers, bestaande uit militairen, politie en eigen personeel hoefde ditmaal niet handelend op te treden.

Dutch newspapers and TV channels gave extensive coverage to the amazing scenes in the centre of Amsterdam and my appearance there was even covered on Pathe News

ZANGER DAVE BERRY GEKOOID

Dave Berry vlucht voor vurige fans

(Van een onzer verslaggevers)

Amsterdams bereden en gemotoriseerde politie moest zaterdag op het Museumplein charges uitvoeren tegen enkele duizenden tieners en honderden kleuters. Het waren de wanhopig teleurgestelde fans van tiener-idool Dave Berry, die zijn belofte om een koppel duiven op te laten moest breken.

En het begon zo rustig.....

ZWOLLE — Dave Berry is geweest. De tocht van Buitensociëteit naar Grote Markt was rustig. Meisjes achter kantoorramen wuifden, enkelen hingen een bord met „We like the Stones" buiten. De boerenkapel „d'Heigeneimers" blies vrolijke deuntjes. De open caleche met de heer A. Boelens, directeur van de nieuwe grammofoonplatenzaak die Dave Berry zou openen, zijn dochter, Dave Berry zelf en één van diens gitaristen klepperde kalm voort. In de Luttekestraat stonden de trottoirs vol teeners. De rijweg lag open. Dave zou per bakfiets van de oude zaak in de Voorstraat naar de nieuwe honderd meter verderop in de Luttekestraat rijden.

Er kwam niets van.. Toen de koets op de hoek Grote Markt—Voorstraat verscheen, vloeide de massa samen tot één brullende, tierende menigte. De paarden steigerden, de boerenkapel blies door, de politie voerde een hopeloze strijd. De stunt met de bakfiets werd afgelast. De bakfiets werd later vernield teruggevonden.

Bloemist Vroom — tegenover de nieuwe grammofoonplatenzaak — „De Artist" — zal elke keer als hij Dave Berry hoort zingen, terugdenken aan de dag van gisteren toen enkele teeners door zijn etalageruit werden gedrukt, toen hij aankeek tegen een vernielde verwarmingsbuis, gebroken vazen en verfomfaaide bloemen. Andere middenstanders in de Luttekestraat zullen zich herinneren dat zij die twee gekke uren niets hebben verkocht en

Schools and workplaces closed for the day when I visited the Dutch town of Zwolle to sign a few autographs

There was bedlam when I made another public appearance too. Performing in the northern Holland town of Zwolle with The Cruisers, I was invited to do an autograph signing session in a record shop. I was led around the town in a procession with trumpet players from a local band and the town's schools, which knew all their kids were planning to play truant to see me, closed for a day's holiday. Some local workplaces also closed and there were again thousands of people out in the streets hoping for a glimpse of Dave Berry.

Whenever I have returned to Holland and Belgium throughout my career it has always been a fantastic experience. Kids who were fans in the sixties have stuck with me down all the years and through their lives. I have always been grateful for their support and I enjoy making myself available to meet them whenever I can.

Dave Berry stops the show in Belgium

THE British star of the recent Teenbeat Festival at Ghent, Dave Berry, literally stopped the show. This extraordinary young artiste got such an acclamation from the audience of 7,000 that things got completely out of control, and the show was stopped by order of the police. Dave is undoubtedly one of the greatest showmen of the moment, for he has a strange and almost hypnotic effect on his audience. He has a rare and curious brilliance that must be felt to be understood, and when the enthusiasm of his fans becomes unreasonable, this can be understood by those who are present. Much of what he has goes into his discs, but a personal appearance of course gives even more.

This great Festival, one of the biggest of its kind ever to be held in Belgium, took place in the huge Palais des Sports at Ghent on November 13, and to say that it was merely a success would be an understatement. More than 30 big Belgian and international stars and groups were there to take part, but owing to the show ending unexpectedly some were unable to appear.

Marc Aryan, sharing the honours with Dave Berry, got a tremendous ovation. This young composer-singer of Armenian origin is now one of the Continent's big stars, and he will go far. His songs please people of all ages, especially young people, and he has a enjoying tremendous success in Belgium and elsewhere lately with a recording of one of his compositions called "Early Bird," still very high in Belgium's Top Ten charts. His style is decidedly more sophisticated than that of the beat groups proper, but it has a very wide appeal.

Of the beat groups proper participating in this Festival, several must be mentioned. The top favourites in Belgium at the moment are The Jumpers; they were chosen to accompany Dave Berry, and also appeared separately. Very international are The Flying Condors, who, although they are at present based in Germany, are actually made up of an English boy, an American, a German and a full-blooded Sioux Indian who is Canadian. They wear Red Indian costumes, and their performance is acrobatic as well as musical, but the youngsters love every moment of it.

Peter Welch and The Jets appeared at first in clown costumes, and even with green faces, and they too went down well. Later on they come on in more normal garb, and were just as well received, for they give what their special type of audience want and expect. The popular Sirtaki dance was presented by the Duo Acropolis from Greece, and from the Netherlands came The Phantoms.

As to the music played at this

Police stepped in to bring a premature closure to my 1965 performance in Ghent, reported here in The World's Fair

BELGIANS PUT BAN ON BERRY SHOWS

BRITAIN isn't the only country facing a cash crisis—Belgium's also bothered and all because of Dave Berry!

Dave, whose "Mama" hit the Belgian and Dutch Top Tens this week, has earned so much from his huge following in Belgium that the government there have ordered a restriction on the number of concerts he plays to reduce the amount of money being taken out of the country.

But Dave is booked for Belgian dates at St. Nicholas (August 26) Liege (28) and Hoiblaait (29), besides an Ostend appearance (13), before taking a two-week Spanish holiday (September 3-17).

G.B. STARS ON BELGIAN T.V.

Dave Berry is to host an all-British TV pop show in Brussels next month. **Tom Jones**, the **Fortunes**, **Paul and Barry Ryan** and **Twinkle** are also on the show on March 27.

The programme comes at the end of Dave's three-day visit to Belgium, during which time he will also star in concerts. Earlier, he flies to Paris on March 11 to do four TV shows, breaking his visit to return to Birmingham to tape ABC's "Lucky Stars" (13).

He stars with the **Animals** at Paris Olympia on March 15. Dave and the **Cruisers** have been added to the **Herman's Hermits-Mindbenders-Pinkertons** tour which kicks off at Dover ABC on April 7.

Meeting Belgian fans (top) and continuing to have my name in the newspapers

Opposite: Keeping fans at home informed

Other European countries have also made me extremely welcome and in 1970 I had the honour of representing Malta in an international song festival featuring dozens of performers in the beautiful former Yugoslavian city of Split. I had performed in concert in Malta two years previously, but for the life of me I can't recall how I came to be singing the Maltese entry in such a prestigious competition. I do remember the event had a complex and bizarre format where I sang a song which was then translated into Serbo-Croat for someone else to perform. Then other nations' songs were translated into English and I was given the new words to learn and then perform as well as I could.

Another South Yorkshire singer, Tony Christie, was also there and goodness knows which country he might have been singing for. Singing sisters Sue and Sunny also featured. They were a well-respected session duo working with the likes of Tom Jones and Lulu and they were Joe Cocker's backing vocalists on *With A Little Help From My Friends*.

Not quite so welcome in Split was *She Wears My Ring* performer Solomon King, an 18-stone one-hit-wonder who thought he was God's gift. He was so full of himself and complained endlessly when he was asked to learn new songs. It was as though he was the only one who was being requested to do any work and when I asked him what he was moaning about he just said: "Dave, you are a really nice guy but if you don't shut your mouth I will smack you with this beach chair."

It's the only time I can ever remember any other performer threatening me in such a way but we rejoiced because we had finally found a way to prompt a natural human response from Solomon. On another occasion in Manchester, the American was performing in a huge nightclub and behaving in his customary manner, treating people without any respect whatsoever. It's not a wise way to behave in the entertainment world and the musicians in the house band gained their revenge for his rudeness by changing key when he went into a solo section of a song, then switching back to the original key for the remainder of the number. It left Solomon singing in the wrong key and completely stranded and although he was aware that something was going on, he couldn't be certain what had happened.

Dave Berry and The Cruisers
Fan Club Newsletter

Hello again,

Once again Josie has asked me to let you know what's been happening to Dave and the Cruisers during the last month.

First of all Dave went to Belgium for a week, where he appeared in the largest hall in Brussels for one week. We had a fantastic time and on the opening day 40 policemen were called in to control the fans. It was really frightening because over there the police have guns and they look very powerful. The show ended with the police firing their guns in the air and the manager carrying Dave off the stage.

Meeting Marthy

THE continent presented me with much more than fame and hit records; it also introduced me to my wife-to-be, Marthy, who I first met in Holland on October 1st, 1965. Then called Marthy van Lopik, she worked for a TV company and through her job she had first seen me on stage at the Knokke Festival.

We met at an event for performers and other showbusiness people which was hosted by the Dutch Decca people at the time of the Grande Gala du Disque. I remember her telling me how much all the film crew had enjoyed my performance at Knokke because it had been so different. Wayne Fontana was with me that night and, together with Marthy and a friend of hers, we went out as a foursome until seven the next morning. To this day, Wayne still tells Marthy that she chose the wrong one that night!

Shortly afterwards, I was with a business colleague, Geoff Cantor, staying in wonderful hotels in Lisbon and Estoril. It was time for us to return to Britain but I said I would not be travelling back with him. Marthy was on my mind and I knew she was the one for me so I suddenly changed my flight plan and headed back to Amsterdam to see her again. Marthy had certainly had a strange effect on me... and I liked it.

Opposite: Grabbing a Dutch souvenir during an Amsterdam photo-shoot

Right: Marthy and I stuck a pin in a map of Europe to decide where to fly to on holiday

I was always playing games with the Press and nothing changed when I married Marthy in 1967

The year 1965 was a very special one and meeting Marthy was the icing on the cake. I was single, had been on the road for six years and had known several girlfriends but no-one I had fallen for completely. However, Marthy and I hit it off instantly and I knew straight away that this was something special.

I flew to Amsterdam to meet her to go on holiday together and in the airport's VIP lounge we did what many couples can only dream of; we closed our eyes and stuck a pin in a map of Europe to decide where to spend our first holiday together. The pin landed on Greece and a representative from Schipol airport arranged a flight, a hotel in Athens for a couple of days, then trips on to Crete and Rome.

I remember how excited I was flying to Amsterdam to meet Marthy's family for the first time. They were always very nice to me even though it must have been difficult for them having a man they had seen on TV appear in their home and then, the following year, take their daughter to England to live. But we were in love and nothing else mattered.

We have always loved travelling and in our first year together enjoyed wonderful times in Naples, America and Canada. On a holiday flight to Spain, I waited until our 'plane had reached about 20,000ft before I produced a ring and asked her to marry me. Our wedding was a semi-secret affair at the Register Office in Weston-Super-Mare. I had frequently visited the Webbington Country Club nearby which myself and the band used as a kind of bolt-hole for a couple of years. Marthy and I liked the West Country and we thought the club would be a wonderful place to celebrate our wedding. After the official ceremony we went back there with her family who had flown over from Amsterdam, the band members and a few other friends. We enjoyed a lovely meal and someone had booked a local band from Bristol to play for us. Members of the Press were around but they didn't get any pictures of us.

I was thrilled to be marrying Marthy although I was also a little concerned what the fans would think when they heard the news that I was no longer a bachelor. It sounds ridiculous these days, but no-one in the 1960s knew what was to become of pop stars who married. Our wedding was a very special event indeed... and the next day Marthy found out exactly what it was like to be married to a singer when I went off on a tour of Scotland.

Drink and drugs were never a threat to our marriage because I never had very much to do with them. Both were available, but while I could stay up drinking with the best of them until 5am, I know when to stop. I always like to stay in control and you can't do that with drugs.

I am so proud that Marthy and I have been married for more than 40 years. We have always been independent people but when we're together, we're very together and when we are apart I always look forward to seeing her when I return home. We enjoy a special life together and one of the main things is that we continue to have a laugh.

Dave is a bashful groom

By Ray Wood

Pop star Dave Berry is definitely married.

I found out the truth last night after a day of rumours and denials.

Dave's own manager denied Dave had wed. His road manager denied it.

His publicity man, Kit Wells, was completely surprised when a Western Daily Press reporter spoke to him about it in London.

And the man who could solve the mystery, Dave himself, was nowhere to be found.

Nor was the new Mrs. Berry — 22-year-old Dutch girl Marty van Lopik.

But last night, Alan Wells, of the Webbington Country Club, confirmed that Dave was married—and had spent his wedding night at Webbington.

Dave has known Marty

DAVE BERRY
Shy pop star

about a year. He met her in Amsterdam during one of his frequent visits.

Dave is shy, and wanted to avoid the typical show-biz wedding with all the circus atmosphere.

At the week-end he quietly moved into the Webbington club.

His parents came down from Sheffield, and Marty arrived with her parents from Amsterdam.

Also there were Dave's backing group, the Cruisers.

Then on Monday afternoon they all went to Weston-super-Mare town hall, for the wedding.

And yesterday the newlyweds left the club

Destination: shsshh.

Pop star's 'wedding' mystery

Mystery today surrounded the "wedding" of pop singer Dave Berry, reported to have taken place yesterday secretly at Weston-super-Mare.

Dave Berry, in his real name of Dave Grundy, was said to have married Dutch girl Marty von Lopik, and the couple were reported as starting their honeymoon at Webbington Country Club.

But at the club the singer's road manager strenuously denied the wedding. The couple, he said, had merely been in the West Country for "a party."

song?

MARRIAGE? IT'S DONE ME NO HARM says DAVE

DOWN in zyder country the other day somebody stirred for a change . . . and the secret of Dave Berry's marriage to Dutch girl Marty van Lopik in dormant Weston-super-Mare was out. The telegram delivery boy recognised that the groom, Mr. David Grundy, was in fact pop star Dave Berry.

Mr. Berry and bride immediately went to ground and nobody got around to any interviews with the happy couple. Presumably, it was supposed, because Dave wasn't so happy with all his fans having found out.

by BOB FARMER

So does he believe pop stars should be bachelors? "Actually, I don't agree with that at all," he argued. "It's done me no harm so far as I can see. I've even received lots of congratulatory cards from the fans. It's great when your fans react like this.

"I think people underestimate the intelligence of teenagers. They are a lot more intelligent than people give them credit for.

"Take publicity. You can give someone a really big build-up, but this won't guarantee the teenagers liking him. It depends entirely on his ability and the standard of his record."

Monkees

But Monkee-baiters would be the first to question the intelligence of teenagers. People like P. J. Proby for instance. "The Monkees made it because of their TV show. People in show business are jealous of their sudden success, but I don't think the same applies to the public. Remember the early days of the Beatles? Show biz was just as jealous then."

Since the interview was straying from the subject of marriage, Dave agreed to explain why, as he doesn't believe marriage affects the fans, he kept his wedding so secret.

"I just enjoyed the chase. Between me and everybody else. I like a bit of drama. The idea of running away to Gretna Green appeals to me, but I couldn't do that. So I did the next best thing and waited to see how long it would be before people got wind of what I was doing. I knew, after all, that the marriage would leak out in the end."

As an additional wedding present, he's hoping for one of those rareties — a Dave Berry British chart entry with his new single "Strangers."

On the Continent, of course, he's enormous. Here at home, he's never even had two successive hits. "Mama" was his last big British success, but the inconsistency doesn't cause him much heartache.

"I can go a year without a hit because I'm not judged on the chart. I've got a stage act that people remember. Just because I haven't a hit doesn't mean people won't come along to see me.

Bitter?

"So I'm not at all bitter towards Britain. Actually, I find it a rather nice situation. In the old days, pop stars just got up and sang. They had nothing else to offer. Today, you've got to have some sort of presentation because the fans won't accept you otherwise."

Cruisers Roy Leger, Pete Cliffe, Roger Jackson and Alan Taylor

A much later Cruisers line-up featuring , from left, Jason Wood, Nip Healey, bass player Jo Wadeson and Brian Wood

Stage Stunts

Working on my image as The Prince of Darkness

THE Cruisers are probably deserving of a place in The Guinness Book of Records for having the largest number of members down the years. There must be about a hundred musicians out there who can say they have played in Dave Berry's backing band at one time or another. Most of them tended to stick around for a while - a couple of years at least - and a handful have been with me for a large slice of my career.

In addition to being talented musicians, some of them were real characters too. Pete Thornton was the first guy in the band who had real style. Within an hour of us checking into a hotel he would be showered, changed into an Italian suit and the pair of us would be relaxing in the bar with either a whisky and dry ginger or a bourbon and 7-Up.

Fellow Sheffielder Frank White has always been highly respected by many leading performers and other people in the industry. When he joined The Cruisers in the 1960s it was not only his playing ability which people admired; he also had an eye-catching double-necked solid mahogany Gibson guitar which he had imported from America which added a little more mystique to our performance.

My band members became used to me making unusual stage entrances, often delayed, as I began

'SHOCK' RECEPTION FOR POP SINGER

ALTHOUGH "POP" star, Dave Berry proved to be one of the most popular artistes ever to appear at the Winter Gardens his Banbury fans were in fact lucky to see him at all.

Little did the hundreds of screaming teenagers know that Dave was still suffering the effects of a severe electric shock from the previous night's performance.

As hordes of girls clambered to reach his dressing room, Dave was whisked away to the Whately Hall Hotel where he talked about the incident.

He said: "I was giving a performance in a club at Bristol when suddenly five girls grabbed the microphone from my hand and as a result the amplifers broke down.

Blue flash

"We then had to resort to the club's equipment, and as I was doing a number there was a big blue flash. That's all I remember," he said.

His road manager added that Dave sank to the floor and was unconscious for about 20 minutes.

"Despite spending most of Thursday in bed Dave is still very shaky," he said.

Pop singer Dave Berry goes through his arm-waving act—standing just out of reach of the outstretched arms of his fans.

During his performance, twenty-three-year-old Dave, who comes from Sheffield, sang about a dozen numbers including his big hits, "Crying Game", "Little Things" and "Memphis Tennessee".

Supporting

On the 17th of this month, Dave, who has now been singing professionally for three years, will be going to Belgium for a three-and-a-half-week tour, which will include a number of television appearances.

Supporting Dave were Banbury's New Astranaughts, an amalgamation of the Rooks and the "old" Astranaughts, and a very good sound they provide too. Also The Siftas, a young local foursome.

P.W.

I always carefully plan my stage entrances but a 1965 show in Bristol saw me making a shock exit singing in the wings before eventually being picked out by a spotlight. It became a kind of trade-mark as I teased the audience into guessing where I might appear from. However, at one show I very nearly didn't appear at all...

There were three clubs on the River Trent known as The Yacht Clubs and one night I planned to leave from the back of the dressing room, climb onto an outside fire escape and have my roadie pass me a microphone before I climbed up the steps to make a dramatic entrance. I was hanging onto the fire escape with one hand, holding the mike with the other and was halfway through singing my first song when I tried to open a fire door to walk onto the stage. But it stuck. The band must have thought I was just messing about because they were soon into the second song of the night with me still outside singing while clinging to the fire escape. It must have lasted for five minutes or so before I finally got through the door.

Another inconvenience came at a gig in Devon when, for a bit of fun, I decided to make my entrance from the door of the ladies toilet. Just before we were introduced I nipped inside the doorway, ready to walk out into a spotlight when the music began, but for some reason there was quite a delay and I was trapped in there with lots of women and girls walking past me to use the loos.

Some entrances have been nothing short of spectacular, however, and one of my grandest was at the old Tyne Theatre in Newcastle. Stage managers and lighting engineers often remark how much they enjoy working with me because I like to make unusual entrances and at Newcastle I was shown a trap-door in the stage. It was the kind of device usually saved for the pantomime Genie but I agreed it could be a dramatic start to the show.

It was controlled by an old wind-up device and, just like me, it worked so slowly. Two men were needed to operate it and I was told to strike a pose, stand perfectly still, and wait to make my appearance through the stage floor. I didn't tell the band, of course, and the guitarist and bass player couldn't believe their eyes when my hand suddenly rose through the dry ice which was swirling around their feet. They almost couldn't play for laughing.

Another entrance which took a good deal of courage came at The Embassy, Skegness, where, with the help of stage crew, I climbed to the top of a huge ladder which was hidden from view behind the curtain at the side of the stage. When I began to sing, I held out my arm into the spotlight and the audience must have thought I was 18ft tall. Ever so slowly, I was helped down the ladder's rungs, still singing, and although I could hear other musicians roaring with laughter at the back of the hall, there was hardly any reaction at all from the audience; it was as if they saw that sort of thing every night of the week.

The one thing I always wanted to do on stage, but was never allowed to, was to not appear at all. People knew my act and were always expecting something different so I thought it could be a tremendous piece of performance art to stay in the wings and sing, teasing the audience with my fingers picked out by a spotlight, perhaps holding my bracelet. I talked it through with TV show floor managers but they were not at all keen on the idea.

There should always be a little magic and mystery from a performer and I always keep myself out of sight of the audience before my shows. One night I went to see American jazz legend Billy Eckstine at The Fiesta in Sheffield and was in the bar enjoying a drink an hour or so before the show was due to begin. I was amazed when Billy walked in, casually dressed, and ordered a drink for himself. It was as if a spell had been broken and it spoiled the night for me.

A magical piece of stagecraft I fully appreciated was by Gilbert Becaud at the Paris Olympia when I went along with Marthy. As an encore, all the backdrops were completely removed from the stage, leaving just a bare wall, a ladder or two, a tin of paint and a few other theatrical items. As one of Gilbert's most famous songs was played he just strolled onto the stage as if no-one was there, lit a cigarette and relaxed as he smoked it. It was as if we were all watching him unwind after his performance. I made a mental note to try something similar after one of my own shows.

I received fan mail from far and wide but letters from one particular young lady always stood out. Judy Eggleton, a schoolgirl from Nelson in Lancashire, embellished the backs of her envelopes with elaborate artwork often depicting lines from my songs

YOU'D BETTER MOVE ON
THE CRYING GAME
JOHNNEY B. GOODE
THE HOOCHIE COOCHIE MAN
B
D
B
D
MISTER RHYTHM AND BLUES
EVERYBODY'S TRYING TO BE MY BABY
MEMPHIS TENNSEE
HEARTBEAT

The Hoochie Coochie Man PART one
a gypsy woman told my mother
before I was born
"you've got a boy child coming"
he's gonna be a son of a gun
he's gonna make all you pretty women
jump and shout
and the worlds gonna know
what it's all about,
well you know I'm him,
everybody knows I'm him
well I'm the Hoochie Coochie man
everybody knows I'm h.m

Track 14

Sister Act

MY younger sister Julia was very much a child of the sixties and an original "rock chick". She was there by my side from the beginning, supporting my band at all our gigs both large and small, and when success came along she was a part of it, sharing some fabulous experiences with me. Julia, just two years younger than me, often accompanied me when I went to TV studios to do shows such as *Ready Steady Go*. She dressed like me in all black and everyone knew she was my sister. We even did a TV programme together, appearing with Peter and Jane Asher talking about relationships between brothers and sisters.

In addition to her going out with Mike McCartney, she was also Adam Faith's girlfriend for a time. I remember one day going on a shopping spree with Julia down London's most fashionable roads, Oxford Street and Carnaby Street, accompanied by Roger Daltrey and Pete Townsend from The Who. We were looking for clothes to wear for our TV appearances and visited all the fashionable and famous boutiques such as Mr Fish.

JULIA GRUNDY is Dave Berry's sister and very proud of the fact, too.

"It's funny," said Julia, "but when we were children Dave and I weren't particularly close. You know what brothers are like when they're young; they chase you about and tease you.

"Well, it was just like that with us. Then when we had grown up a bit and got into our teens, we became very close. Now he always sticks up for me and won't let anybody boss me about or anything."

I asked Julia if she had kept anything of Dave's from their childhood.

"Oh, *everything*," she said, "all his football books for instance. He was mad on football, still is, and his stamp collection. He was very proud of that."

"Do you buy Dave's records?" I asked her.

"Mum does," said Julia. "She usually buys two of everything, so that we can play one and keep the other. We like to have souvenirs of Dave's career. They'll be nice to play in the years to come."

"Do you see Dave very often?" I asked her.

"Very often," she said. "When I know he is going to be late home from a show I wait up for him, so that I can see as much of him as possible."

"Does he remember your birthday?" I asked.

"He never forgets," she said. "Also, when he knows I'm going away on holiday or something he usually gives me my spending money and insists that I take it. Last year we went to Majorca together, it was gorgeous."

"Do you travel around with Dave a lot?"

"As much as I can, yes," she said; "and they are very good about it at work." (Julia is a professor's secretary.)

"Really, you know," said Julia thoughtfully, "he's not like a brother at all—more a very good friend."

London was a very special place in the swinging sixties but I was never tempted to live there. My agent Danny Betesch was - and still is - based in Manchester and I once asked him if he thought it would be necessary for me to move to the capital. We decided that there was so much interest in music which was coming out of northern cities such as Liverpool, Manchester, Newcastle and Sheffield, plus Birmingham in the Midlands, that it certainly was not a necessity. Indeed, in 1963 and 1964 there was even a spell when it might have been detrimental to my career to have been based in the south.

Me and my shadow...Julia and I out shopping on a grey day in London's Oxford Street

When my European popularity took off, my feet hardly touched the ground as I travelled between cities such as Paris, Antwerp, Brussels, Rome and Copenhagen so it didn't really matter where my home was. Julia left to live in Geneva and my other sister Mary moved first to Newcastle and later to complete a degree at London University, but I was happy to live near to my roots and remained at the family home in Beighton until I was 26. Most of my friends were still in the Sheffield area and I remained close to both my mum and dad right until they died.

One place I would have loved to explore was the USA but my record sales never took off across the Atlantic. Don and Phil Everly had told me to get over there, saying my act would go down incredibly well with the Americans but it just never happened. Wayne Fontana and The Mindbenders, Freddie and The Dreamers and The Searchers all went. Looking back, while British acts were doing 80-odd back-to-back shows across the States on Dick Clark's Bandstand tour, eating junk food and drinking Coca-Cola, I was working my way around the old capitals of Europe, lapping up the culture, staying in wonderful hotels, dining in all the best restaurants and singing in magnificent theatres where legends such as Edith Piaf had performed. I don't think I missed out.

BALLET FOR DAVE!

POP PICKING

DAVE BERRY telephoned from Amsterdam yesterday with a great story.

Said Dave: "I had been booked to do a spot at the Cassino in Knocke le Zoute, a Belgian holiday resort.

"When I reported to the Casino, huge posters screamed down at me 'All Star Ballet, featuring Dave Berry!'"

It took half an hour before it was all sorted out.

There was an evening of ballet at the Casino—a big charity event. But that started at 9 p.m. Dave had been engaged for the pop warm-up which began at 8 p.m.

Sheffield's Dave is currently No. 1 of the hit parades in Belgium and Holland, with "Strange Effect," which surprisingly made little headway here.

London was a special place in the 1960s but I was never tempted to live there. Europe became my pop playground and despite the occasional misunderstanding (left) I was thrilled to perform there

DAVE TO PLAY IN PARIS

BEIGHTON pop star Dave Berry has been booked to play at the largest theatre in Europe, the Olympia in Paris, along with the British top group The Animals.

Dave Could Be A World-Beater

by DAVID HALL

He's the lad who still hasn't been exploited to the fullest. He's tall, handsome—and yes, even dark, just like in the fairy stories. He sings differently, he dresses differently, he has a different stage act, and he even manages to make his whole image appear mysterious and different. I suspect that if some bright, enterprising spark put him on American TV and did a good job on promotion over there, he could be the biggest sensation since Elvis made the rounds some time ago.

His name of course is Dave Berry and I have quite deliberately chosen to write about him again in a matter of weeks because I feel that this young man isn't getting the exposure needed. He is certain, in my eyes anyway, to become the biggest thing since Cliff Richard in Great Britain and if he plays his cards right and doesn't just have himself exposed as a Top Twenty singer as he is at the moment, then he could suddenly become the biggest and most in-demand star anyone has ever known for the last few years.

I doubt very much whether anyone has really thought about Dave Berry in the way he should be thought about. At the moment he is still treated as one of our better pop singers and that's about all. But he has the unique triplication of a different voice, or rather different style, a different stage act, and a different face, all of which have made people like Elvis Presley and Cliff Richard the stars they are.

You can somehow sense the star talent in Dave Berry and you can feel it too, especially when he is on-stage and putting over his act to the best advantage. But I feel he is being killed off at the moment through the wrong sort of publicity, or rather that the public are getting the idea that Dave Berry is just another pop singer who doesn't mean anything. Anything except the fact that he is a Top Twenty star, which although very commendable isn't the best thing when he could become a second Elvis Presley.

I'm not the only one with this verdict. Quite a few thousand fans are believing that Mı. Berry could suddenly spring a surprise on the nation and whip into the charts in double-quick time not only here but in America and also start himself really spinning both in films and on TV and he could hit the big-time in such a way as to really excite the nation.

There are some artistes who have star written all over them from the day they are born and Dave Berry is one of these. He has a new single out and it's likely to be another smash hit for him, but I'm still rather sad that this star should be so underrated as to be just a Top Twenty name and that no one has really seen the depths in him which should be probed and put to the test as to whether he can get into the Big League side of Pop with the Elvis Presleys and the Cliff Richards.

DAVE BERRY

Godfather of Punk

Exploring options for the future, I took to the stage in a production of Expresso Bongo

MOST bands and singers had initially signed up with their record companies on three-year deals so 1966 was a time of reckoning for many who, like myself, had broken through in 1963. The taxman had caught up with some performers, others had suffered a big dip in their popularity and many discovered that their impressive record sales had not been converted into money in the bank. To learn they were also being released by their record companies was a huge blow. A number of outfits who were no longer having much of an impact on the charts discovered that when it came to negotiating new contracts they had very little bargaining power.

My own big UK chart successes were behind me too but 1966 turned out to be rather a special year and one which set me up financially and professionally for the rest of my life. It all hinged on my massive popularity on the continent where I had five records riding high in the Dutch and Belgian charts plus other successes elsewhere. The timing was extremely fortunate and I reasoned that I was in a strong enough position to not only sign a new contract with Decca, but also to negotiate a healthy pay advance with them.

I startled Danny Betesch when I told him I planned to ask for £20,000, a considerable amount in 1966 when you realise I had just bought a house for my mother in Beighton for £2,100. Danny said Decca would never pay me that kind of money and he was right. Nevertheless I was well pleased with the £18,000 they did agree to. I had big outlays at the time and had to fund my own recording costs of £3,000 for the next three years but, recently married, I now had financial security whether or not I went on to sell any more records. I could plan for the future and make my own decisions.

Marthy and I had been living in a flat close to Sheffield University but we were able to move to a large, attractive house beside a golf course in Dronfield, Derbyshire - a home we have gone on to share for more than four decades.

Neither money nor fame was the driving force for me. I got my biggest kick out of waiting for the charts to be published on a Tuesday and reading my name in the same listing as Elvis Presley. No amount of money could possibly match that kind of thrill and I clearly recall the first time I met the Everly Brothers and thinking to myself "is this real?".

However, I did wonder just how long my career in music might last so I looked around for other avenues to explore. One of my ideas was to get into acting and in 1964 I accepted an invitation to take to the stage in a production of *Expresso Bongo* at Westcliff-on-Sea, playing the role of pop singer Bongo Herbert which had been made famous at the cinema by Cliff Richard. The production ran for two weeks and was very successful. Although I thoroughly enjoyed the experience I found it hard work, mainly because I had continued with my gigs during the time I was rehearsing.

I later enrolled on an acting course in London with a view to going into films and did appear in one movie, *The Ghost Goes Gear*, in 1966 along with The Spencer Davis Group and Nicholas Parsons. Thankfully I continued to be in demand as a singer so although the acting had been an interesting diversion, I didn't have to take it any further; I simply realised that I was a musician and not an actor.

Now it's the acting game...

DAVE BERRY, the 23-year-old pop star from Beighton, near Sheffield, has been signed to play the lead in a London stage production of Expresso Bongo.

"I couldn't believe my ears when I was asked to take the part — I just burst out laughing," said Dave today.

He will play Bongo Herbert, the expjloited young singer, in Wolf Mankowitz's play. Cliff Richard took the part when it was filmed a few years ago.

TRIAL WEEK

Several singers were in line for the part — including Adam Faith — but after seeing Dave several times on television producers decided on him.

"The play goes on for a sort of trial week in April and I will start rehearsals a few weeks before," said Dave. "After that I don't know what happens."

"I've no ambitions in this direction. Basically, I'm a singer and that's what I like doing, but this is something different and I will try anything for a short time."

"I've only been in school plays before, but I'm sure I shall enjoy this."

Acting was an interesting diversion but I continued to be in demand as a singer

As the sixties turned into the seventies, it was certainly a period of transition for me. My chart successes had been and gone, I swapped record companies from Decca to CBS and, although I retained much of my popularity on the continent, the scene was changing here in Britain.

In the music world there is a saying that popularity comes and goes in ten-year cycles and that was certainly the case with me. The fourteen and fifteen-year-olds who had screamed at my concerts in the early sixties were now twenty-four and twenty-five, mostly married with young children and mortgages to pay. It was a time for them to look back on their teenage years and reflect on what they had enjoyed... and perhaps to consider what they were missing. An astonishing number of the kids who had screamed at me in ballrooms up and down the country now returned to see me on the cabaret circuit.

I took to performing cabaret with a great deal of enthusiasm because many aspects of the work suited me down to the ground. I was thrilled at the interest people had retained in my music and my stage show and I generally enjoyed a tremendous audience reaction. The smart venues were very impressive indeed with first-class lighting rigs including follow spotlights which were ideal for my act. Being based at one venue for as long as six nights at a time with plenty of rehearsal time available, there were real possibilities for me to develop my act.

The seventies and eighties were decades of transition for me... and I'm amazed my fans could recognise me behind all that hair!

28 DAILY EXPRESS Wednesday March 1 1978

Twenty years at the top...a Eurostar supreme

DAVE BERRY

Berry: 'On stage I'm mean and wild'

Family man — Berry with wife and daughter

The eternal handyman of pop is the godfather of punk

Report by Trevor Reynolds

NEW wave music owes more than a small debt to 'sixties star Dave "Boots" Berry. It was the sinister, almost evil presence of Berry, which gave Punk rockers the gloves, scarves, boots, chains, leather gear and all-black rebel image.

Berry, now 35, is Holland's top solo singer. He is a big name in Belgium and at £1,500 a week is a European all-round rock star. Bad boy Berry, the Woodhouse-born son of a retired property repairer, is big business. And he's got style.

Dave, whose latest single, "Night of the Fly," is due out soon, is riding on the crest of success with a fat £25,000 record contract.

Twenty trend-setting years at the top and Dave still hasn't a shred of grey in his mop of black hair. And today's

I went from performing on the cabaret circuit to being labelled as The Godfather of Punk

I performed for cabaret audiences from Dundee and Edinburgh in the north to Brighton and Portsmouth on the south coast, giving audiences some of my hits and some rock 'n'roll, and for much of the time it was like being on a paid-for holiday.

Anyone observing me enjoying the comforts of the cabaret world would no doubt have been surprised to see newspaper headlines soon afterwards proclaiming Dave Berry as "the Godfather of Punk". One evening at a rock venue in London I was astonished to notice some very odd-looking characters at the front of the stage. The punk era had just arrived and although I was delighted to see some of them enjoying my show, I couldn't quite work out what the attraction was for them. My road manager ushered them to my dressing room, saying they wanted to meet me, and my question to them was straight to the point: "What are you doing here?"

They said they were fans of the Sex Pistols and had noticed that they were doing some old Dave Berry B-side recordings, including *No Lip*. Another band, The Monochrome Set, were performing a version of *Little Things*. Adam Ant, who started out as a punk, had given me a name check on the back of his first album, saying I had influenced his career, and Siouxsie and The Banshees were also fans.

Punk was more about attitude than anything else -

just like rock 'n' roll - and I was delighted that some of these exciting new performers had been aware of my act.

Adam Ant respected me so much that he invited me to support him and his Ants at a few shows when he was extremely popular, starting at The Lyceum in London's Leicester Square. The reviews I received were very special indeed and my daughter Tania couldn't believe it when I took her along to meet Adam. Even better, I received my punk badge of honour when the audience spat at me on stage!

Also in the 1970s, just as I had once imitated Gene Vincent, other acts had clearly been influenced by my stage performances and copied what I did. I knew Alvin Stardust when he performed under the name of Shane Fenton. He came from Mansfield, just a few miles down the road from me, and when he re-invented himself in the 1970s he wore black leather, gloves, stood still on stage and cavorted with the microphone in his hands just as I did. It was quite clear that he had based his new image on the way I performed on stage.

I was in a show with him several years later at Lincoln Castle and before we began I went across to him in the dressing room. "Let's get one thing straight from the start," I said to him. "Can we establish which one of us will be doing my act tonight?" He didn't laugh.

When my agency asked me in 1976 what I would think of performing in Rhodesia, I thought for a moment that they were talking of a tiny village of that name close to Worksop, just a few miles from where I grew up. But it was a two-month trip to the African state they were offering me and I jumped at the chance - even though it meant leaving Marthy at home with our daughter Tania who was only seven or eight at the time.

I appeared in a huge nightclub in Salisbury, accompanied on stage by half-naked dancing girls,

My act went down extremely well in Rhodesia but some of the things I witnessed in the country left me feeling rather uncomfortable

My adventure in southern Africa was certainly exciting but after two months I was ready to return home

and the venue was full of ex-pats who were all keen to talk to me about my music and career. I was amazed to find the town just like Salisbury in Wiltshire, complete with Marks & Spencer and familiar-looking banks and other businesses on the high street. It was as if a corner of England had been transported to Southern Africa.

The owner of the nightclub I worked at was Indian and he invited me to his house on my day off, serving me some wonderful food. However, this was a time of extreme political tension in Rhodesia - later to become Zimbabwe - and I was appalled at the apartheid system that existed.

At one show I met a man who was from a suburb of Sheffield called Frecheville, a place I had performed at many times. Although he worked as a simple motor mechanic in Rhodesia, he had a large home complete with a swimming pool, gardeners and a housekeeper. It was an amazing lifestyle but, in common with most black people, his staff were treated like dirt. I was angry to see this and any right-minded person would have felt the same way. It was clear that such an unfair system simply could not and should not last and it was a big education for me to see it in operation.

It wasn't a lifestyle I adapted to very easily at all and I felt particularly uncomfortable when I reflected on how I had been brought up on black American music which had its roots in the days of slavery in the Deep South. Although I did not enjoy many social aspects of the trip, there were unforgettable highlights including visiting the spectacular Victoria Falls on a day off and flying over the Kariba Dam with my road manager, John Adams. Such adventures were tremendously exciting but after two months I was certainly ready to return home.

Dave Berry

dave berry

Dave Berry

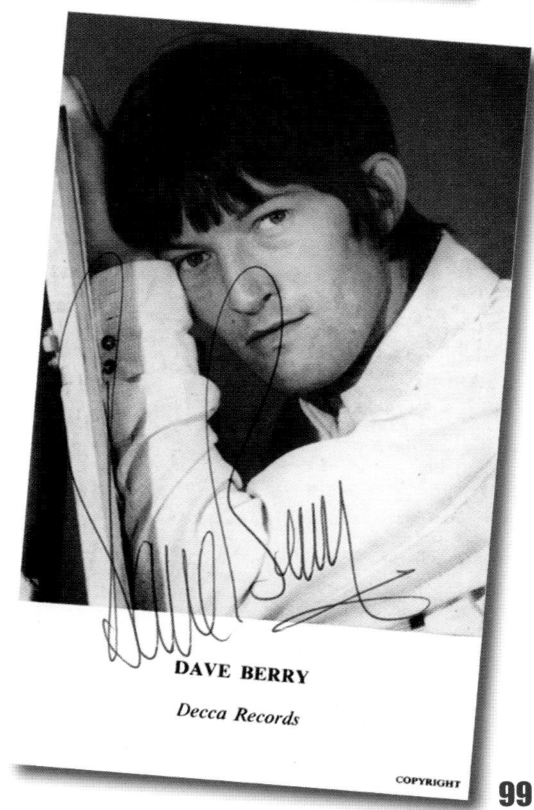
DAVE BERRY
Decca Records
COPYRIGHT

A dedicated follower of fashion

KNOK
MME
Coup

SHIRE POST

LEEDS THURSDAY OCTOBER 28 1971 PRICE 3½p Tel. LEEDS 32701

'This Dave Berry is not the father of my child'

Yorkshire Post Reporter

A WOMAN told last night how she examined the forehead of Dave Berry, the pop singer, and decided he was not the father of her child, born last December.

Mrs. Wendy Brook, 29, had earlier applied for an affiliation order against Mr. Berry, at Ossett, West Riding, Magistrates' Court.

Mrs. Brook, a hairdresser, said at her Goring Park Avenue, Ossett, home last night that after she had examined Mr. Berry's hairline she decided he was not the father of her child.

"The Dave Berry I knew had a mole on his forehead. This Mr. Berry has not.

Apology

Singer 'cleared' by a mole

By GILBERT JOHNSON

A YOUNG redhead looked for a mole on pop singer Dave Berry's forehead yesterday — then decided he was not the father of her baby.

... hairdresser

POP STAR BABY CASE DROPPED

Daily Telegraph Reporter

A WOMAN withdrew an affiliation summons against Dave Berry, the pop singer, after she saw him in court yesterday. She admitted that she was mistaken.

Mrs Wendy Brook, 28, a hair dresser, drew back the singer' long hair, and discovered tha he did not have a mole on his forehead. The "Dave Berry" she knew had a mole, she said.

Ossett, Yorks, magistrates heard that Mrs Brook alleged a man claiming to be Mr Berry was the father of her nine-month-old illegitimate son.

'Drastic mistake'

After the hearing, Mrs Brook, of Leopold Street, Ossett, said: "I am completely foxed. I just do not know what to think. The Dave Berry I knew was short and had short hair. He had a mole on his forehead."

After the hearing, Mr Berry, a six-footer, of Highgate Lane, Dronfield, Sheffield, said: "It is all a drastic mistake. Today is the first time I have seen this woman.

"The only answer is that a mystery Mr X is posing as me. I can't think who he is, or why he should pick on me."

Dave was not the villainous Mr. X, says redhead

REDHEAD Wendy Ann Brook looked for a mole on Sheffield pop singer Dave Berry's forehead—then decided he wasn't "the villainous Mr. X" who made love to her in May last year.

'He had such a charming voice—I guess it was

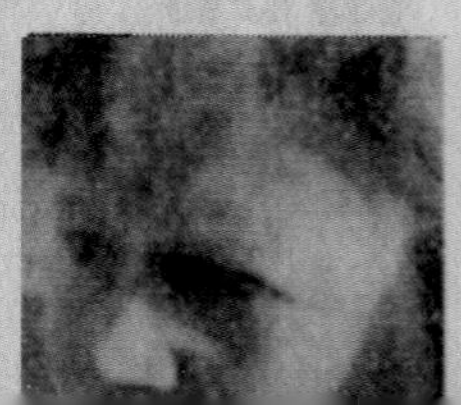

Brook that he would be away in Germany for a few months.

"During that time," she said, "I never once went out with anyone."

They started going out together again and in May this year they met in Wakefield. After walking round the town they were

Dave Berry and his wife after the hearin

Showbiz hazard—Dav

The Lying Game

NOT everyone who pressed a piece of paper into my hand was after my autograph. When two people approached me before a 1971 cabaret performance at Batley Variety Club, I assumed they were fans but they were waiting at the stage door to serve me with a writ.

A hairdresser called Wendy from nearby Ossett had claimed that I was the father of her baby son and she was determined to take me to court to prove it in a paternity suit. It was an allegation I could certainly have done without, but it was such a ridiculous claim that I was not unsettled for long.

She alleged that her first date with "Dave Berry" had been to a cinema in Doncaster when he told her he was a divorcee and wanted them to become engaged. Cilla Black was going to be on their wedding guest list and Dickie Valentine would be best man.

I had never heard of this woman, let alone met her at any time, and I had the proof because on the dates she claimed she had been with me, I had been on tour in Scotland, staying in a hotel in Kirkcaldy. This information was passed on to her legal people but they didn't want to know and pressed on with taking me to court. My solicitors suggested getting everyone together for a meeting, at which it would have been clear to the woman that someone had deceived her, but again they wouldn't hear of it. They must have been convinced about her allegation and clearly thought I was just a pop star trying to get off the hook.

So off we went to appear before Ossett Magistrates where I was curious to see what this hairdresser looked like. Once the redhead was pointed out to me I knew for certain that I had never seen her before in my life. The case was adjourned for a few minutes during which I was asked to lift up my hair at the front. Apparently the man she had known, claiming to be me, had a mole on his forehead and when she couldn't find one on my face she realised she had made a huge mistake.

What really astonished me about the whole affair was that the fellow who duped her, always referred to in court as "the villainous Mr X", was a short man who wore suits - hardly my image at all. I never heard whether the imposter was ever traced but he was certainly someone who had it in for me... quite literally.

Just as I had never known the hairdresser, I don't ever remember meeting a Redditch nightwatchman by the name of Roger Cole, but he clearly knew quite a bit about me. The first time I heard his name was in 1989 when two CID officers from Birmingham knocked on my door and showed me an autographed photograph of myself.

Mr Cole had assumed my identity to impress a woman he spoke to on a telephone chatline service, a deception which only came to light when his employers received a telephone bill which was around £17,000 more than it should have been. Over a spell of three months this man had regularly telephoned a lonely housewife called Lynn whose lorry-driving husband worked nights. He claimed to be "Dave Berry", wrote the woman a song and even sent her a genuine autographed picture of me.

Detectives were curious as to why my signed picture had been posted to the woman but once I explained that I gave away hundreds at my shows they were happy and went away. I didn't hear anything else about it until a few months later when the court story was splashed across the front page of *The Sun*. The whole thing was quite bizarre and, once again, I was left wondering why someone had chosen to impersonate me.

NIGHT GUARD RANG UP £17,000 CHAT BILL

By MARTIN STOTE

NIGHT watchman Roger Cole's smooth telephone patter was a hit with a bored housewife.

He told her he was Sixties pop star Dave Berry. And in a string of nightly chat-ups he held her spellbound with tales about his life of fame.

He sent her signed photos of the singer — autographed by himself — and rang pretending to be in Barbados. He even offered her tickets for his concerts.

Cole, 38, wrote the woman a song, and gave her a girlfriend telephone number on which he left a bogus taped message from "Dave Berry's fan club." In all, star-struck Cole blew £17,000 of his firm's money by talking to girls on chat lines, Worcester Crown Court heard yesterday.

His shocked bosses

THE Sun

Wednesday, January 17, 1990 22p Yesterday's estimated sale: 3,948,477 Thought: Call this winter?

£17,000 BILL FOR CHATLINE ADDICT

Bomb in mail for general

EXCLUSIVE by JOHN KAY

THE IRA yesterday launched a new terror blitz, sending a deadly letter bomb to the Army's top sports officer.

A Jiffybag packed with enough explosives to kill was addressed to Major General Alan Yeoman, director of the Army Sport Control Board.

CHATLINE nut Roger Cole made £17,000 worth of calls — all on his FIRM'S phone.

In five months, the lonely nightwatchman rang up bills of up to £1,000 every week.

A typical call lasted one hour 44 minutes. At 25p a minute, that's £26.

And Cole, 38, was on the blower eight hours a night seven days a week — sometimes using five phones at once.

He bombarded lonely night worker's wife

5-month spree on firm's phone

By JOHN SCOTT

It was also established that when Cole was off work sick for four days,

ashamed and embarrassed, but it was purely a friendship.

"My husband works nights and I got fed up watching TV,

Night worker who said he was singer Dave Berry rings up a £17,000 bill

By AUBREY CHALMERS

NIGHTWATCHMAN Roger Cole spent hour after hour on his employer's phone calling a Chatline number, pretending to be Sixties pop star Dave Berry.

In three months he is said to have cost the firm about £17,000.

Cole sometimes had all five lines engaged simultaneously on the controversial 25pence-a-minute Chatline.

Frequently at the other end of the line was housewife Lynn Brassington, 21, whose husband works nights. Cole convinced her he was Berry, whose hits included The Crying Game and Little Things.

Last night, after the fictitious pop star was unmasked, he said: 'All I have is a sore memory which makes me feel ashamed and embarrassed. I feel very foolish.'

Autograph

Cole bombarded her with calls at her home at Stoke-on-Trent, claiming at times to be ringing from Barbados.

He wrote her a song which he played down the line, gave her the number of his 'fan club' and even sent her an autographed photograph of Berry — which he had signed

Lynn Brassington: 'Ashamed'

period it was accepted that of the total bill of £19,000 some £17,000 was attributable to unauthorised use. He said the vast majority was attributable

My Pop Pals

Still friends after all these years... a reunion with PJ Proby

WHEN performers are together they usually get along just as people from other walks of life do. We talk about our experiences of course but we don't generally sit around backstage chatting about stardom or showbiz. There is only so much you can discuss about music and bands.

We all have our own particular interests so other performers are just as likely to ask me about antiques or walking as they are about music. I know Chris Farlowe was trained as a joiner and furniture restorer specialising in art deco, so I would probably talk to him about that.

I remember once after a show at The Royal Concert Hall in Nottingham I was in the dressing room with my friend Adam Pemberton and Mike d'Abo of Manfred Mann. We were on a long tour and were sipping cups of tea when one of them told us that he had taken his cat to the vet's in the afternoon. Then someone else in the show confided how he was concerned about his dog which had also been to see the vet with a problem.

Then we all put down our teacups and laughed out loud, agreeing how ridiculous the scene was; after all, we were hardly living up to our industry's "sex 'n' drugs 'n' rock 'n' roll" image, were we?

I always got along well with PJ Proby - Jim - who was, and still is, a great character and a special rock 'n' roll performer. I toured with Jim when he first arrived over here from the States in 1964 and our paths still cross occasionally, 45 years on.

In the late 1960s Jim was living for a time at the Manchester home of Wayne Fontana and his wife. Wayne went out to do a show one evening and returned to find his home empty; Jim had disappeared and so had his wife. Many years on from this I found myself on the same bill as both PJ Proby and Wayne Fontana and a puzzled Jim sought me out to say he just couldn't understand why Wayne wouldn't speak to him. "Well," I reminded him, "perhaps it has something to do with the time you ran off with his wife."

The Small Faces were always great fun to be on the road with and, looking back, I suppose I might well have beaten Rod Stewart to the role as their frontman. I enjoyed an unforgettable night with the band in Denmark in the late 1960s after I had performed at the Tivoli Gardens in Copenhagen. Band members Stevie Marriott, Ronnie Lane, Ian McLagan and Kenney Jones were working over there for a TV show and we met up after we had all finished for the evening. We decided to visit a local rock club where there was a great atmosphere and I ended the evening singing a half-hour set with them. Rod joined the band just a few months later... but it could have been me!

Speaking of Rod, I remember something he said one Saturday morning when I was in a hotel room watching him on a Tiswas-type programme. The presenter interviewing him enquired, "What would you have been doing this morning if you hadn't come in to the TV studio?" As quick as a flash, Rod replied that he would have probably been at home enjoying a cup of coffee and a slice of toast. Just like most other normal people.

Those who think shows and concerts are glamorous can never have been in one. Most theatres are dumps backstage and the performers enter through a stage door which is usually down some dark back alley. There are only a handful of venues which are exceptions to this rule, such as St David's in Cardiff and the Royal Concert Hall in Glasgow which are magnificent places to work.

The most glamorous part of the business these days is that you get to travel around in nice vehicles, you can eat in excellent restaurants and you stay in good quality hotels. It is all a far cry from how things were in the 1960s when travelling around Britain was extremely difficult, places to eat were hard to find, particularly on Sundays, and hotels were few and far between.

The production might look wonderful to the audience but shows are often not quite as glamorous for those taking part

When Dave Berry came to Manchester, my friend and I went to see him at Belle Vue. With a lot of pushing we managed to get to the front, right up against the stage. Everybody was trying to get hold of him! When he sang "The Crying Game" he hid behind a massive plant.

All of a sudden a girl near the front grabbed the plant and Dave had to release it. I managed to get a leaf of it before a man took it from us. I couldn't get Dave's autograph, so I've stuck a bit of the leaf in my book instead.—Hilary Tidswell, Hyde, Cheshire.

The maverick in me is attracted to making journeys between gigs in the dead of night

Worldwide Gigs

THE great New Orleans performer Louis Armstrong once caused a sensation when he appeared at Batley Variety Club in West Yorkshire. When a journalist asked him why he was doing his show there, his reply was "because they wanted to pay me". I once put the same question to Humphrey Lyttleton when he appeared at a nightclub in Rotherham with Helen Shapiro and he answered, "If someone contacts my agent, asks if I'm available and they agree a contract, then I will appear anywhere."

It has been exactly the same with Dave Berry and The Cruisers and we have performed at any number of strange venues down the years. One of the oddest was a sports hall in Holland where I sang in a boxing ring with my band members completely out of sight outside the ropes. At another leisure venue, this time in Scotland, we performed at the side of a swimming pool with the audience on the other side of the water, having hardly any connection with us at all.

Organisers of a Round Table charity garden party in Kent provided a stage which had been converted from a hay waggon and then in Australia I entertained sheep farmers at a woolshed in Yallah, a town in the middle of The Outback.

When it comes to lunatic gigs, I have certainly done my fair share. Fortunately, I have always derived a kind of perverse pleasure from travelling around the country in the middle of the night, skirting around towns and cities on dark motorways when everyone else is fast asleep in bed.

Sometimes when I inspect the schedule of a long tour I will look at the travelling involved and although most gigs are carefully planned there are usually instances of being in a town such as Blackpool one evening and then maybe at a concert hall in Folkestone the following night. The maverick in me is attracted to making such journeys in the dead of night and this also gives me time to meet people around the country who I have known for many years.

For instance, if I find myself in Dundee one night and in Newcastle the next, I might well take off after the first show and head for a friend's hotel I know in Jedburgh, arriving around 2am. I will get up late in the morning, perhaps buy a couple of tasty haggis from a nearby butcher's shop I know and then continue on my way to Newcastle.

The strangest gigs all seem to have arrived in more recent years and the most bizarre of all came when I punctuated a six-night pre-Christmas run at a fabulous hotel in Usk, South Wales, with a one-nighter in Hong Kong. The Welsh hotel had booked me to appear for three nights, followed by three days off at the weekend and then returning for three further performances.

Out of the blue, a promoter asked me if I would be interested in travelling to Asia to sing one night in Hong Kong, followed by another show in mainland China. I explained that I was already booked to appear in Usk but when we had a close look at our schedules we realised I would be able to complete the Hong Kong leg of the trip during my three-day break. It was going to be an extremely tight schedule but the promoter was keen to get me on his Hong Kong bill and he very kindly agreed to pay me for doing both shows, even though I would not be continuing on to China.

Phil Oakey took Sheffield back into the charts in the 1980s with his band The Human League

I went straight to bed after my third performance in Usk and a taxi called for me at 5.30am the following morning, whisking me off to Heathrow Airport. With an eleven-hour flight and a time difference of eight hours, I was already disorientated when I arrived in Hong Kong. Another taxi collected me at the airport and I arrived at a stunning hotel on the harbour side at 6.30pm local time, just three hours before I was due on stage. The show was split into two sections, from 9.30-10.30pm and 12.30-1.30am, and by the time I got to bed I had no idea what day it was.

Fortunately I had a full day to recover before flying back to Britain on the Monday morning and the time difference meant I finally returned to Usk in the early afternoon, well in time to have a sleep until 7pm and then perform later in the evening. As I checked back into the Welsh hotel a member of staff walked over to me and said: "Hello Dave; have you done anything this weekend?"

I continued to travel to gigs both near and far in the early 1980s, an era which saw the building of several big arenas with capacities of 12,000 or so. I had been well used to performing for crowds of 2,000 at concert halls so it was a big step up to appear at places such as the massive Sports Palace in Antwerp. I also began playing with a new generation of performers including another excellent Sheffield band, The Human League. The 1980s was a great time for music, but then again I can't think of an era of music I haven't enjoyed. I'm not too keen on rap but I love dance music and if I had been 17 or 18 I know I would have been at the all-night raves.

It is great fun touring the country with other stalwarts of the 1960s

The 1980s also saw me embark on tours of West Germany and in one memorable month I performed for ten days in Abu Dhabi with The Swinging Blue Jeans before returning to do shows in Aberdeen and Liverpool and then at Hallowes Golf Club in Dronfield - only a hundred yards from my home.

Then came a renaissance in 1960s music with the birth of the Solid Silver 60s tour featuring a number of acts and a formula based completely on nostalgia. The show remains extremely popular to this day and I am delighted that, together with my guitarist Brian Wood, I will feature on the tour for its 25th anniversary year in 2010. The Troggs, Brian Poole from The Tremeloes, Peter Sarstedt, Mike Pender of The Searchers and The Swinging Blue Jeans are also on the bill. With around sixty dates planned during three months on the road, some people have told me the schedule looks daunting but I have retained the same appetite for performing that I had all those years ago. Singing live still excites me and it is always a fantastic feeling to know I am going on tour.

In addition to appearing at Sheffield City Hall once again, another highlight of the 2010 tour will be a date at London's Royal Albert Hall. I played there in 1968 and I must have been really good because it has taken them just 42 years to have me back.

Wayne Fontana was responsible for landing me perhaps my most glamorous gig in 1997, a three-week adventure on the QE2 liner where my backing band lived up to their Cruisers name as we sailed around the Caribbean. Wayne had appeared on the liner himself and put my name forward to his agent.

I took Marthy and our daughter Tania along with my band, sound engineer and a couple of their girlfriends and we lived in the lap of luxury; in the 21 days afloat we were only required to perform three times. Other celebrities on board included BBC reporter John Simpson, Jilly Goolden, Carol Thatcher, Riverdance performers and the comic Jim Bowen. There were also several well-known authors meeting guests and doing on-board book signings. One of the highlights of the trip was a VIP reception for all the entertainers with the captain and his fellow officers.

I was to re-acquaint myself with the QE2 in 2002 when a former agent of mine, Derek Franks from York, took the *Reelinandrockin* show to the Southern Hemisphere. Other performers were Gerry Marsden, Mike d'Abo, Brian Poole, Mike Pender and The Nolans.

With a band of cruisers on board the QE2, from left, Brian Poole, Mike d'Abo, Dave Dee and Mike Pender

Keeping my birthday celebrations afloat are, from left: Mike Pender, Wayne Fontana, Tony Crane, Dave Dee and Brian Poole

Another picture with a nautical theme but this one, with Gino Washington, was taken a little closer to home at the 2007 Dartford Regatta

The whole adventure began with a week-long stay in Jersey before we flew to New Zealand to pick up the QE2 in Auckland. Once on board we performed for guests as we sailed across the Tasman Sea. I'm not usually a person for reflecting on the past but as we arrived in Australia, sailing close by Sydney Harbour Bridge and Sydney Opera House, it did cross my mind that all this was happening to "Sugar" Grundy, the lad from Woodhouse.

We travelled by air between Sydney, Brisbane, Adelaide and Perth and did ten shows. It was my first trip Down Under and I was a little apprehensive because my music had never made much of an impact in the Australian charts. I need not have worried, however, as the Aussie crowds were fantastic to me. Many of the characters out there were very off-the-wall and because my act was slightly screwball they took to it straight away.

A highlight came in Sydney where we were given an official reception and there was another "I can't believe this is happening to me" moment when we relaxed on the balcony, sipping cocktails and looking down on Sydney Harbour.

I was soon to get a close-up view of the Bridge when I took time out to climb all the way to the top. The initial part was the scariest, scaling a ladder with the road and water hundreds of feet

Meeting a couple of fellow entertainers on the QE2, Nolan Sisters Maureen and Anne

With another celebrity on board the QE2, Jilly Goolden

CLIMBER CERTIFICATE
This is to certify that
DAVE BERRY
successfully climbed to the summit of
the Sydney Harbour Bridge
16 June, 2003
BridgeClimb
FOR THE CLIMB OF YOUR LIFE!
Paul B Cave
Founder & Chairman

Enjoying a spectacular view of Sydney Harbour with tour production manager Steve Ellerington and (inset) my certificate

beneath me. Tied to a runner-rope, I asked one of the stewards if it would save me if I fell. "No, not really," he reassured me.

On the way back to the UK, we stopped off for a one-night performance in Singapore and were again treated like royalty, being invited for drinks with diplomats.

It is fortunate that I enjoy travelling so much, whether it be around Britain, Europe or the world. I have visited some very special places indeed but sometimes when Marthy and I have been on holiday it has not been possible to entirely get away from my career.

In the early eighties, during a trip to America, we visited Niagara Falls and were taking in the spectacular scenery when up alongside us pulled a coach full of Dutch tourists. Someone recognised me instantly and for three-quarters-of-an-hour I was just as big an attraction as the Falls, signing autographs and chatting to fans. As for the Americans patrolling the Canadian border, they just looked on bemused with no clue as to who the hell I was.

They say it is a small world and there was another example when I returned to Australia in 2003. Back at Sydney Harbour, I heard someone say, "Hey Dave, what are you doing here?" It was a couple who lived just around the corner from our home in Dronfield and we were saying hello to each other on the opposite side of the planet.

Threat to Career

I SURVIVED a serious threat to my career in the mid-1990s before going on to enjoy perhaps the most satisfying stage of my life as a performer. For several weeks I had been aware that something was not quite right on stage, complaining first about our monitor system and then the sound set-up. I could not quite work out what was wrong but eventually I realised the problem was with me.

Pub licensee Len Badger, the former Sheffield United and Chesterfield footballer, had once introduced me to a customer of his who was an ear, nose and throat specialist at Chesterfield and North Derbyshire Royal Hospital. I dropped in on Len to see if he would ring his friend on my behalf and, within an hour or so, I found myself sitting in his kitchen where, with no specialist instruments at hand, he went to his cutlery drawer and stuck a spoon down my throat to aid his examination. His prognosis was that nodules had grown on my vocal chords and I was shattered, fearing that my career was at an end.

I was admitted to Sheffield's Royal Hallamshire Hospital where the nodules were removed using laser treatment and to aid my recovery I was told not to attempt to speak at all for three days. I remained extremely concerned and for the first time in my career I had to cancel a number of bookings. I was out of action for a couple of

When I had to cancel shows because of a serious throat problem I feared it might be the end of my career

Memphis . . . . in the meantime
KELLY'S
MARKET
dave
BERRY

My Memphis.... in the Meantime CD was the first time I had been able to properly plan the content of an album

months and my recuperation programme involved sessions with a voice coach.

Thankfully the operation was successful and I was recommended to continue with vocal exercises when I returned to performing. It might sound ridiculous to people when they hear me going through my loud routine, but I carry on with this therapy before every performance.

One night in a hotel in Corby I was performing my vocal exercises in my bedroom before leaving for a show when the phone rang. It was the hotel manager who sounded very concerned about me. Apparently two young girls had been alarmed at loud noises they had heard, reporting that there was an extremely drunk man in the room next to theirs.

I enjoyed a great feeling of satisfaction in the 1990s when I returned to my roots, performing and recording my beloved blues and R&B. Having achieved national and international success as a singer of pop songs, people might have thought it a strange move for me, thirty years on, going back to the style of music which had initially influenced me as a teenager. I was very much excited at the prospect and initially appeared at The Rockingham Arms Folk and Blues Club in the village of Wentworth, near Rotherham. I was rather apprehensive but the audience gave me a fantastic response and they have gone on to welcome me back every year since. The venue has changed in recent years but I thoroughly enjoy performing there.

Alexis Korner had been regarded as the father of British blues and he was someone I had always looked up to. When I learned in 1995 that a memorial concert in his name was to take place at Buxton Opera House, I really fancied being a part of the tribute which was being organised to raise funds for his widow. I simply telephoned the organiser, explained my interest and asked if I could become involved. Straight away he said "yes".

Having been added to the bill at a very late stage, many of the dedicated blues fans in the audience turned up for the show not knowing of my involvement. I was again apprehensive, wondering if I would be accepted and had the exact same feeling of tension I had experienced all those years ago when I started out on my career. Thankfully, many of the people in the audience were aware of my roots in the blues and some even knew that I had been on the very first British album recording with R&B in the title - along with Alexis Korner. They gave me a fantastic welcome and it was as if my career had been reborn.

I continued performing my hits with The Cruisers but word quickly spread that I was back doing the music I loved, so when we included songs by Billie Holiday and Muddy Waters into our set once again my career had effectively turned full circle.

Van Morrison invited me to appear with him at some of his concerts; not simply doing a guest spot but performing the whole first half of the show for him. Once again my appearance had not been advertised but R&B fans are particularly loyal and appreciative and they knew that if Dave Berry was on the bill it was because Van Morrison wanted him to be there.

Again the response was very enthusiastic, so much so that it encouraged me to return to the studios in the late 1990s to record a brand new album, *Memphis.... in the Meantime*. Although I had sold hundreds of thousands of LPs in my years with Decca and afterwards, they had chiefly been compilations of my hit songs, together with B-sides and other tracks from recording sessions I had done. This was the first time I had been able to treat an album as a project in its own right and carefully plan its content. I chose wonderful songs by classic writers and recorded the album in the Exeter University studios backed by the talented band, Junkyard Angels. One of the tracks, J.J. Cale's *Cajun Moon*, received particular attention, reaching No 1 in the chart on DJ Mike Reid's Radio London internet station.

In 2003 I took to the road with a show called *A Shot of Rhythm 'n' Blues*, being joined by The Animals, The Troggs and Zoot Money who, incidentally, had also appeared on that initial British R&B album way back in 1964. One remarkable thing I noticed was that, just like in the early 1960s, fans were curious to know where some of my songs had come from. To have them asking such questions after I had been a performer for almost half a century was one of the greatest compliments of all.

The early years of the new millennium also saw the launch of *Reelinandarockin*, the first ever properly produced 1960s music show. Appearing with stalwarts Gerry Marsden, Mike Pender and Mike d'Abo, we shared the stage and sang harmonies together. The show ran for six years and took us to Singapore, Denmark and Sweden in addition to Australia and for some reason it changed my attitude towards my own performances. I lightened up a little and began to not take myself quite so seriously. I made a few little asides on stage to make fun of myself and the audience seemed to love it... so I have been doing the same ever since.

Many bands and performers who have survived from the 1960s have hardly changed their shows at all down the years, performing the same old music in the same old way. Some I can think of can't have learned a single new song in more than 15 years. That was never going to happen to me. It is important not to alienate your fans by doing too many new songs but people appreciate my set because it is always different. Keeping the show fresh also ensures I am never on automatic pilot and throughout my career I have always had half-an-hour or so to myself before going on stage in order to go through things in my head. I am happy to have talented young performers working on stage with me; they also help to keep my performance fresh and I am keen to listen to their opinions.

When I am singing with a band, the first priority is to play music for ourselves and it is important that we are happy with what we do. Secondly, I am always aware that there will be other musicians watching the show so they are the next group of people I want to impress, particularly when we are playing something new. If we achieve those two things then the third goal, making the fans happy, usually follows on.

Marthy and I share a passion
for attractive antique
furniture and other items

Going for a Song

I LIVE something of a double life. When I'm not travelling the country to sing at clubs, concert halls and arenas, I spend my time visiting shops, salerooms and auction houses to satisfy my other passion - antiques.

I owe much of my interest in furniture and other collectables to Marthy who has been an enthusiast for many years and also to a former road manager of mine, Eric, who drove the band and our equipment around during the 1960s. Eric dabbled in buying and selling items, often picking up a piece or two from a small outlet in one town, then taking them along on tour with us to sell at a profit elsewhere.

I knew nothing at all about auctions until the mid-1990s when, out of curiosity, I called in to see a sale that was taking place in Saffron Walden. I was fascinated to observe what went on and then I spotted a collection of albums by the great guitarist, Chet Atkins. There were twenty or thirty of them and all appeared to be in mint condition. I had no idea how to bid so I asked the guy running the auction what I should do. He told me to stand where the auctioneer would be able to spot me and simply raise my hand. I walked away with the records for £2 apiece and took them to a record collectors' shop where I sold them on at a nice profit.

After 35 years or so on the road, I had been looking for another interest and I saw the world of antiques as a way of educating myself and also filling in some of my spare time. I had already seen just about every town centre and high street in the country and thought it would be very interesting indeed to buy and sell objects.

Marthy and I took on a small unit at the Chapel Antiques centre in Sheffield in 1997 and it became great fun. Our initial interest in Victorian and Edwardian furniture changed to art deco and art nouveau items and we soon learned how important it was to maintain interest by regularly changing our stock.

Through attending antiques fairs, I have been delighted to meet experts such as Tim Wollacott, David Dickinson and Philip Serrell, being invited to appear on their TV shows six or seven times. Because of my background, I am also occasionally invited to express an opinion when collectables from the world of pop music are offered for sale. Once I was able to offer

Pictured at our Chapel Antiques outlet and (right) with TV's antiques personality David Dickinson

precise information to the BBC and a Sheffield auction house when they quizzed me about an autographed Rolling Stones jacket. I was able to advise them that it was authentic, having been donated by the band and raffled at the Alexis Korner Memorial Concert I had performed at in Buxton in 1995. I even remembered that the raffle tickets had cost £2 each!

I have noticed one striking similarity between the worlds of music and antiques. Just as nowadays it is by far the best time ever for music, with such a mixture of styles, the same is true with antiques where it is now perfectly acceptable to mix traditional items with contemporary ones, such as a Victorian dining table with a couple of modern chairs.

There are other links between antiques and music too. Towards the end of 2009 I took part in a large antiques fair at Lincolnshire Showground and was thrilled to sell a pair of iconic German 1930s Wassily chairs to some Canadian and Russian girls who wanted them for a club they were planning to open in Moscow. Driving home from the fair, it struck me that I would be returning to the same Showground site in 2010, not to sell furniture but to sing in front of 4,000 music fans.

Many people who enjoy my music are well aware of my love for antiques, but it is not necessarily the case the other way around. A female colleague from Chapel Antiques, someone who has known Marthy and myself for several years, told us she had been in a state of complete shock after seeing me being interviewed on GMTV one morning. Up until then she had known nothing at all about about my fifty-year singing career. "To me you are just Dave," she explained to me later.

Recent Times

I HAVE been happy to do a number of performances to support good causes throughout my career and the biggest of the lot has been the annual Rock With Laughter charity show organised by Brummie comedian Jasper Carrott at the NEC. Attracting an audience of around 14,000 enthusiastic fans, it is a very special event, not least because no-one - not even the performers themselves - knows for sure who will be on the bill until they arrive for the show.

I was first invited to take part in 2004 and I have appeared twice since, sharing the stage with Robin Gibb, Lulu, Chris de Burgh, Rick Wakeman, Black Sabbath's Tony Iommi, Bev Bevan of The Move, UB40, The Bootleg Beatles and many others. The show is wonderful fun and it raises huge amounts for worthy causes. I told Rick, Tony and Bev that it was quite OK by me if they wanted to tell their friends they had been part of Dave Berry's backing band!

Meting Mexican film director Ernesto Contreras

Off-stage, a recent highlight was the double-CD launch of *This Strange Effect (The Decca Sessions)*, featuring my recordings from 1963-1966 Also included on there were two very early demo tracks I had recorded with Joe Brown's Bruvvers, produced by Mickie Most. I had not heard either of the songs for more than forty years and thought they were lost for good until one day I received a letter from a fan who had bought the original recordings on eBay from someone in Tamworth. The quality of the recordings was exceptional so they were added to the CD.

Another thrill which came out of the blue was when my version of *This Strange Effect* was selected as the underlying song for an award-winning Mexican film, *Blue Eyelids*. Director Ernesto Contreras had been alerted to the mood of the song by a fellow film director from Sweden and when the movie was screened at the Manchester Film Festival I was invited along as a special guest and was treated like a hero. It really was quite bizarre.

Rocking With Laughter in Birmingham with event organiser Jasper Carrott (top) and funny man Bill Bailey and (right) meeting 'Allo 'Allo star Vicki Michelle at The Marriott Hotel, Regents Park

My fiftieth year as a professional performer saw me travelling down the M1 for three very unusual "gigs".

The first one came about after my local Member of Parliament, Natascha Engel, attended one of my shows. She told me how much she had enjoyed the performance, then a few days later made contact, saying that as she had seen me doing my job, perhaps I would like to travel to London to see where she worked. I jumped at the opportunity and, amazingly, the date I visited the House of Commons with Marthy was the day of Alistair Darling's Spring Budget. All the political heavyweights were there, hanging on to every word from the Chancellor, together with dozens of film crews waiting outside. Goodness knows what role they imagined Dave Berry might have had with the finances of the nation.

I returned to London to see myself being hanged... in the National Portrait Gallery. Back in the 1960s, celebrity photographer David Wedgbury captured a striking image of me sitting in an iconic chair from the time, wearing a stetson. The photograph was used on one of my album covers and now it had been selected as part of a prestigious exhibition, *From Beatles to Bowie - The Sixties Exposed*. It was a huge honour and the official launch gave me an opportunity to catch up with other stalwarts including PJ Proby and Jimmy Page.

There was more reminiscing when I attended a birthday party with a difference in honour of a motorway service station. Watford Gap was fifty years old and I was invited along to represent members of the music world who had been so grateful to use its facilities in the days when motorways had just been invented. Watford Gap, also known as Blue Boar Services, had been a real godsend for us when we travelled around the country in the early hours of the morning after our shows. It was quite a meeting place for musicians and when Jimi Hendrix came over from the States he heard the Blue Boar mentioned so many times that he thought it was a club.

A day out at Parliament with Natascha Engel MP and, below, the image of me which was displayed in the National Portrait Gallery

Still rockin' after all these years... Half a century after turning professional my diary remains as busy as ever

Another survivor of the sixties, Marty Wilde

Appearing on a morning TV show with celebrities including Helen Shapiro, Dave Lee Travis, Twinkle, Tom McGuinness of Manfred Mann, Frank Allen from The Searchers and Brian Poole

All smiles with The Who frontman Roger Daltrey

My friend Mike Pender from The Searchers who I am touring with once again in 2010

Bev Bevan, Robert Plant and Paul Carrack

Lets Dance hitman Chris Montez who I performed with at The Sports Palace, Antwerp

Reunited with Jimmy Page

Nicholas Parsons and Chris Biggins

Meeting Toyah Wilcox

Golden Years

Pictured with the Gold Disc I received for 100,000 sales of my Decca disc This Strange Effect in Holland

BEING a rock star is like being a cowboy. You ride into town, have your fun and then ride out a free man the next day. I've been so fortunate to be able to ride in and out of towns around the world for so long.

None of the performers who emerged in the early 1960s really expected things to last and once I had survived the initial three years I began to believe that, with a little care and attention, I might make a career out of it. Once in the early 1960s I appeared on a Peter Stringfellow bill at Sheffield City Hall with Joe Cocker and a local entertainment critic, Roy Sheppard, wrote that Dave Berry "has an act that will sustain him when his chart days are over."

A nineties Cruisers line-up, Nip Healey, Jason Wood, Brian Wood and Paul Hopkinson

At the time I didn't quite understand his meaning but I now fully appreciate what he was saying.

I have always been proud of the standards my band has maintained and the way we have kept things fresh for our fans by introducing new songs. Some other survivors from long ago play the same old set night after night but we could never do it that way. We respect our audience and I know our fans appreciate the work that goes into making our shows different.

I have never lost the thrill I get whenever anyone mentions my work or gives me a name check. Noel Gallagher talked about me when he was on *The Russell Brand Show*, saying he liked my stuff. I also still get such a kick when I hear my songs played. If it is on *Radio 2* then it is an amazing feeling to realise that there are around six million people listening to it.

Looking around at the current music scene, there are some extremely talented songwriters, singers and bands out there. However, I have no time for two types of performers: tribute bands and those who seek instant stardom through *X-Factor*-style TV shows.

Tribute performers seem to be everywhere, even appearing at festivals alongside authentic bands. I just can't see the appeal and think they are conning the public. If someone ever goes on the road with a Dave Berry and The Cruisers tribute show it would be nothing short of hilarious. I would rather pay my pound to watch a band playing their own music in a pub any day.

As for TV talent shows, can anyone tell me of a quality band that has ever come out of *Opportunity Knocks, New Faces, Pop Idol, X-Factor* or any other such show? And what would have happened to The Arctic Monkeys, Pulp or The Human League if they had attempted such a move? They would not have made it past their first audition.

I don't believe in short-cuts to stardom and I don't believe in luck either; I think you can substitute the word with two others: hard work. Perhaps fate plays a part from time to time but no-one can make a success of any career for fifty years simply by being in the right place at the right time.

When I look back I recognise my life has had distinct turning points including signing my first

Into 2010 with, John Firminger, Johnny Marchetta, Brian Wood and Jason Wood

recording contract and then making the trip to compete in the song festival in Knokke. That event galvanised my career and, of course, it directly led to me meeting Marthy. And to think that at the time I was not really too concerned about making the trip at all.

In recent years, finding myself working in Australia, Abu Dhabi, Hong Kong, Singapore and on the QE2, I have considered how all these things have contrived to happen to "Sugar" Grundy, the schoolboy who was a talkative mischief in class. I suppose the likelihood of me going on to lead such a life would have been nil, really.

Having started out in the 1950s, I am thrilled to now be entertaining people in a seventh different decade. I continue to plan ahead, love having a busy diary of engagements and still enjoy a huge buzz from touring and performing. And if one day the work does dry up, then perhaps I will be glad that I kept my old welding tools.

A reminder of what real work was once like is the box of welding tools I have kept for fifty years... just in case!

Taking the Tube

GIVING some of my songs a new lease of life has been YouTube. I was taken aback to one day discover on my computer two film-clips I did with Frank White for an American TV programme, *Shindig*, in the mid-1960s and had not seen in the intervening forty years.

With tens of thousands of "hits", YouTube sites clearly appeal to many of my long-serving fans and from some of the messages left they have also taken my music to a new generation. Here are some of the comments posted:

babyhowdy233
I remember the late Syd Barrett of Pink Floyd mentioning Dave Berry to me as someone worth checking out. Now I'm finally doing just that and can easily see why Syd liked this guy's music. He is terrific.

random2098
I have been a fan of Dave Berry since the 60s. He has such a haunting voice and beautiful face. And he reminds me of my one and only lost love. Ho hum!

prtmok637
I think Dave Berry is one of our national treasures. He has a huge fan base, has never stopped working and is still a crowd-puller. So why don't we see and hear him on TV? Have the powers that be lost reality as to what the British public want? All too often slots are given to American singers but rarely to our own who are often better. TV planners get real!

lyzzyxy
I hadn't heard of Dave Berry until recently. Wow, he was ahead of his time. I guess the US didn't know what to make of him.

prtmok637
I first saw Dave Berry around 1959-60. He was good then but now he's brilliant. I usually see him two or three times a year. Always makes me feel happy and always very professional. Long may he keep singing. Thanks Dave.

michaelwright999
I last saw him live 1965 in Edinburgh and then the Stones came on at a 500-seater cinema. Great night; how the years fly by.

TheNightlight1
The Crying Game. Forgot how good this is after four divorces.

doctorblue44
This is a very haunting and nostalgic song. I think Dave Berry's version is absolutely brilliant!

Babyhowdy233
OMG I love his shirt! Too sexy!

bertwindon
So should anyone ever ask me again "what is music?" I know just what I'll say: "Dave Berry's *Crying Game*".

Poopaloo55
Atmospheric... brings back memories.

nigelloflaveo
What a great clip. We were only nine or ten at the time and pop mad. We used to parody the way he fiddled with the microphone and twist it using a skipping rope. It was out at the same time as the Zombies' *She's Not There* - two wonderful records, both somehow way ahead of their time.

sixtiesfan007
I saw him two weeks ago on *A Sixties Night Out* in Dudley and in Worcester. Still fantastic.

nostalgiahistoria67
Pure genius! Awesome song!

throovest
This was written by Geoff Stephens. He was the inspiration behind the New Vaudeville Band, among other initiatives. This is a brilliant song and musically unique. The guitar solo was way ahead of its time and Dave Berry is a great performer and got the measure of this spot on.

TonyMahlony
Boy does this take me back! I used to go to Dave's gigs around the Sheffield area back in the early to mid-60s. Also used to meet-up with him, Johnny Tempest and many other local musicians at the Sidewalk Cafe on Saturday afternoons. Great memories!

sallyann1951
Dave Berry is a Sheffield lad, played in my cousin's

pub in the early 60s, as did Joe Cocker. Saw Dave Berry in Salisbury in 1964, along with Billy Fury, The Fortunes, Hermans Hermits and Wayne Fontana - what a list!

arthursmaid

He always used to give me the creeps! He still does all these years on watching this video.

Trulylovelylady

Saw him recently in Manchester. There he was behind a black curtain with a white glove on which came slowly round to the front.... magic! With my girlfriend, now wife, I saw Dave at a club in North Shields in 1966 after this song came out and he did the same curtain entrance, except his gloves were black. I've never forgotten after 42 years. Facinating he still has the same creepy style.

dougputhoff

Great song but the guy's performance was weird.

c9astal9unner

I had my first holiday romance when this was out. I know men are not meant to get all mushy but it still gives me memories

noxinsox1

Way ahead of his time and yet still gigging even now - brilliant.

Uberaoshi

This song totally rocks; the original is always the best!

psychodamned

Love it! He's really sinister. I thought they tried to make him into a British Orbison through *The Crying Game*. And just listen to *Little Things*.

Mark928

Crying Game, absolutely cock on, well done. Listened to for many years, never grow tired of hearing it again.

Mahogany881

I was born in 1980, so forgive my ignorance. I loved this song when Boy George sang it. I've never seen the movie, just loved the song. Well, boy am I blown away by this Dave Berry original; love it! Thanks for the education.

IBertwindon

I "sang" this song all night hiking from Weymouth to Newbury in late '64. Twenty years later I could hardly believe the man was still doing it at Gloucester with The Fortunes and The Searchers.

Freaky JCB

Saw Dave Berry last Wednesday. He was great! I'm only 12 btw.

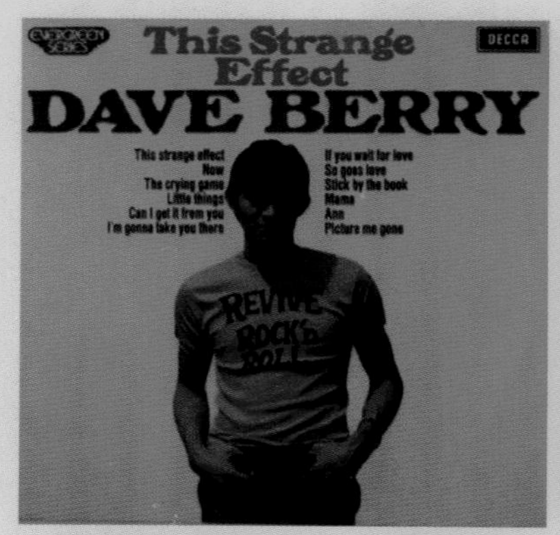
EVERGREEN SERIES
This Strange Effect
DECCA
DAVE BERRY
This strange effect
Now
The crying game
Little things
Can I get it from you
I'm gonna take you there
If you wait for love
So goes love
Stick by the book
Mama
Ann
Picture me gone

this strange effect
dave berry
DECCA

DECCA
DAVE BERRY
THE CRYING GAME
NOT FADE AWAY
ST. JAMES' INFIRMARY
ELLA SPEED GO ON HOME
GOD BLESS THE CHILD
MEMPHIS, TENNESSEE
MY LAST DATE JUST A LITTLE BIT
C.C. RIDER DON'T MAKE FUN OF ME
GO HOME GIRL
THE GIRL FROM THE FAIR ISLE
I DON'T WANT TO GO ON
THE OTHER SIDE OF TOWN
EVERYBODY TRIES

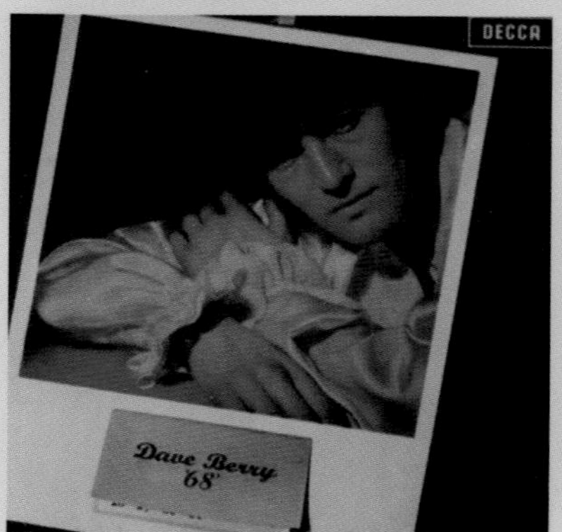
DECCA
Dave Berry
'68'

193.453
THE DAVE BERRY SHOW
Starring: TWINKLE · THE FORTUNES · PAUL & BARRY RYAN · CRISPIAN ST. PETERS · TRULY SMITH
Special Guest Star: TOM JONES
TRULY SMITH
BRT
PROGRAMMATIE: JEF VANDENBERG
REALISATIE: JEF BRUYNINCKX
PRODUKTIE: HERMAN VERELST
DECCA

DAVE BERRY
FOREVER
and I have learned to dream
DECCA

DECCA
DAVE BERRY
mama

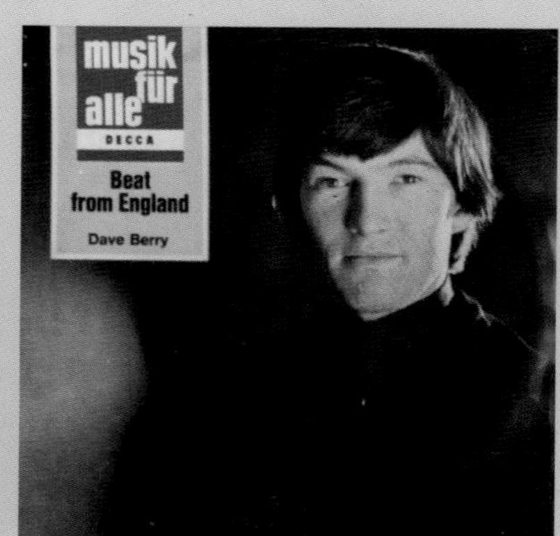
musik für alle
DECCA
Beat from England
Dave Berry

DECCA
MAMA
WALK, WALK, TALK, TALK,

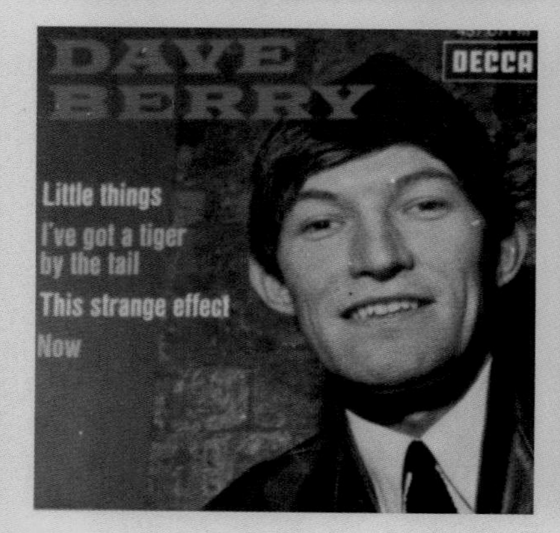
DAVE BERRY
DECCA
Little things
I've got a tiger by the tail
This strange effect
Now

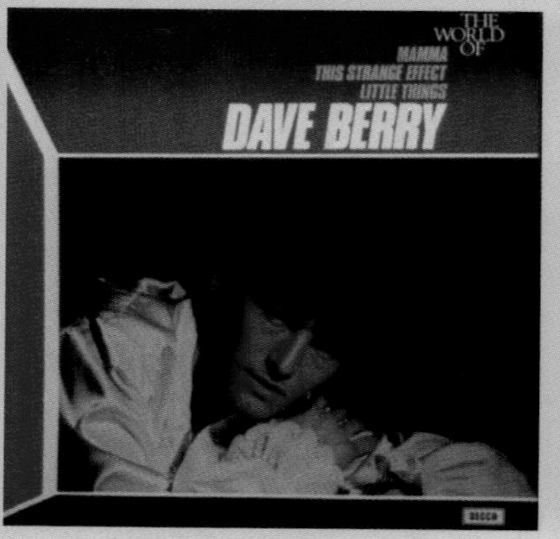
THE WORLD OF
MAMMA
THIS STRANGE EFFECT
LITTLE THINGS
DAVE BERRY
DECCA

the crying game
THE BEST OF
dave berry
DECCA

UK Discography

Singles

Memphis Tennessee / Tossin' And Turnin' - October 1963 (No 19)
My Baby Left Me / Hoochie Coochie Man - January 1964 (No 37)
Baby It's You / Sweet And Lovely - April 1964 (No 24)
The Crying Game / Don't Gimme No Lip Child - July 1964 (No 5)
One Heart Between Two / You're Gonna Need Somebody - November 1964 (No 41)
Little Things - March 1965 (No 5)
This Strange Effect - July 1965 (No 37)
I'm Gonna Take You There - November 1965
If You Wait For Love - February 1966
Mama - July 1966 UK (No 5)
Picture Me Gone - November 1966
Stranger - March 1967
Forever / And I Have Learned To Dream - August 1967
Just As Much As Ever - February 1968
Do I Figure In Your Life? - 1968
Oh What A Life - 1968

EPs

Me-O-My-O / St. James Infirmary / If You Need Me / Ella Speed 1964
Can I Get It From You? 1965

Original Albums

Dave Berry (Decca) 1964
The Crying Game / Not Fade Away / I Don't Want To Go On / Ella Speed / The Girl from the Fair Isle / Go On Home / Everybody Tries / God Bless The Child / Memphis, Tennessee / On The Other Side Of Town / Go Home Girl / My Last Date / St. James Infirmary / Just A Little Bit / See See Rider / Don't Make Fun Of Me

Special Sound of Dave Berry (Decca) 1966
Mama / I Ain't Going With You Girl / It's Gonna Be Fine / You Made A Fool Of Me / Sticks And Stones / Now And From Now On / Same Game / Alright Baby / I Love You Babe / Soft Lights And Sweet Music / Green Grass / Love Has Gone Out Of Your Life / Little Things

One Dozen Berries (Decca) 1966
Hey Little Girl / Round And Round / Casting My Spell / Girl From The Fair Isle / Fanny Man / If You Wait For Love / Sweet And Lovely / Tears To Remind Me / Baby It's You / Run My Heart / I Love You Babe / Heartbeat

Dave Berry '68 (Decca) 1968
Maybe Baby / Coffee Song / She Cried / And The Clock On The Steeple Struck 13 / You Can Live On Love / My Baby Left Me / Baby's Gone / Dying Daffodil Incident / Suspicions / Since You've Gone / Stick To It Ivity / I Got The Feeling

Hostage to the Beat 1988
Searchlight / Love from Johnny / Heart of Stone / Love is a Killer / Bring My Cadillac Back / God Bless the Child / Mountains of the Moon / On the Waterfront / My Baby Left Me / For a Knight to Win His Spurs / Boppin' the Blues / Tracks of My Tears

Memphis... In The Meantime 2003
Mercury Blues / Same Old Blues / Mean 'ol Frisco / Are You Going My Way? / Memphis In The Meantime / Cajun Moon / Georgia Ray / Pony Boy / Taking The Midnight Train / Boppin' the Blues / My Baby Left Me

Compilations

Remembering... (Decca) 1976
The Crying Game (Decca) 1983
This Strange Effect (See for Miles) 1986
This Strange Effect (The Decca Sessions 1963-1966) (2-CD) 2009

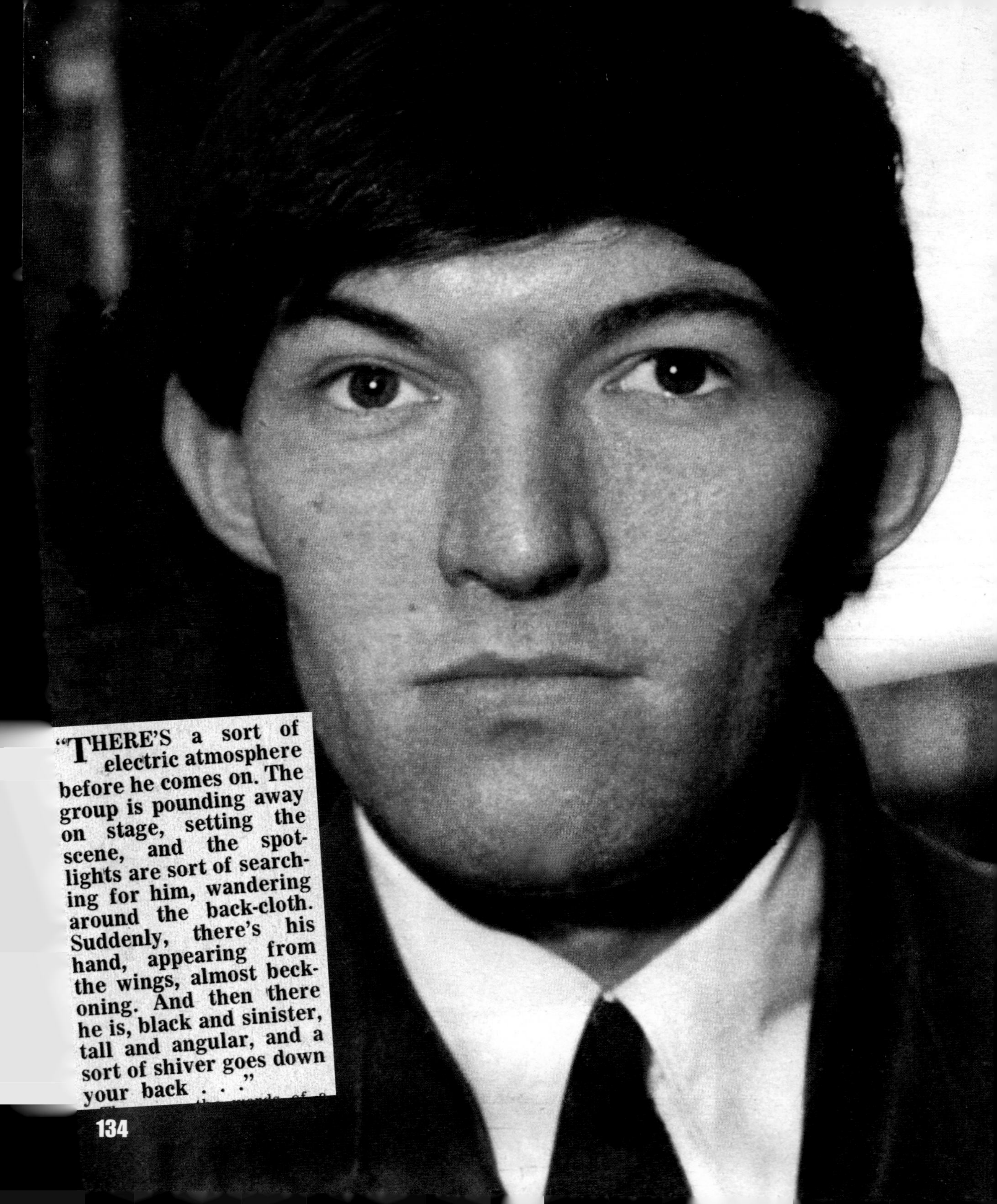

"THERE'S a sort of electric atmosphere before he comes on. The group is pounding away on stage, setting the scene, and the spot-lights are sort of searching for him, wandering around the back-cloth. Suddenly, there's his hand, appearing from the wings, almost beckoning. And then there he is, black and sinister, tall and angular, and a sort of shiver goes down your back . . ."

Backtracking

Bill Wyman

Bill Wyman, Rolling Stones

I FIRST met Dave Berry on Friday, September 27th, 1963, at the Floral Hall in Morecambe, Lancashire. Dave Berry and The Cruisers were third on a bill that included The Rolling Stones and The Merseybeats. I noted in my diary for that day: "Dave Berry did wonderful hand movements with the mike as he sang."

When Dave started out he was just like the Stones and countless other bands from that era in that he covered Chuck Berry's songs. Morecambe was just a week after Dave's recording of *Memphis Tennessee* entered the chart. Two days later we began our first package tour with The Everly Brothers and on some nights we played *Memphis Tennessee*. That's what it was like back then... we were in touch with our roots.

Dave was with the Stones on tours in 1964, along with The Ronettes, and again the following year with The Hollies and Goldie and The Gingerbreads. I was always impressed with his stage act: dressed in black, one hand coming round the curtain, followed by a leg; it all made for a really mysterious show.

Dave inspired many later performers including Alvin Stardust and a number of punk bands acknowledged his importance. Dave Berry is a true original, but one who has not forgotten that the Blues matter.

Joe Cocker, international singer

I FIRST saw Dave perform when I was about 16 at the Frecheville Community Centre in Sheffield. It blew me away. The rhythm The Cruisers laid down was phenomenal. Frank Miles and John Fleet were in that combination and I had great fun working with them years later.

No-one can do Chuck Berry like Dave. He did them all, *Sweet Little Rock 'n' Roller*, *Havana Moon*, *Almost Grown*, singing in a monotone that complemented the band perfectly, weaving around the stage, it was hypnotic.

I opened for him many times at the Esquire Club in Sheffield. I always admired his professionalism, not to mention his dry sense of humour. Let's hope he keeps rockin' for many more years.

Joe Cocker

Peter Stringfellow, nightclub entrepreneur

DAVE Berry and The Cruisers were the first proper band I ever booked. When I began putting on shows in Sheffield, the first two Friday night dances made a loss but then Dave and his band played at the third one... and the night made me money.

The first time they played for me was at St Aiden's Church Hall, called the Black Cat club. I paid them £12 10s and then it shot up to £15 as that is what I paid Johnny Tempest and the Cadillacs. The reason being Johnny and Dave Berry were arch rivals for affection from the Sheffield fans.

Dave was playing Chuck Berry music even before the rest of us knew who Chuck was. He was, and still is, one of the best entertainers in the UK and there was a time when he was even better looking than me. He was always such an impressive figure on stage, dressed in a black leather suit with fringes off the arms. He was so tall that he used to crouch down with the microphone and because he was so skinny and moved with a slow motion walk (he never ever danced) he was nicknamed "Spiderman".

Peter Stringfellow, Frank White and Dave at a reunion at Sheffield's Abbeydale Picture House

Many years later, I booked Dave and his band once again, this time for a birthday party at my Stringfellows club in the West End where they went down a storm. I shall be inviting Dave to play for me at my 70th birthday in 2010.

Chas Hodges... with a new Dave

Chas Hodges, Chas & Dave

DAVE Berry was lucky enough to be born with that eerie appealing flat voice tone. Luckily, also, he had a gift in his blood enabling him to use that voice musically.

My mum, a good musician, was a fan of Dave's. Someone once said to her that he sings flat. She put that person right: "He don't. It's a style unique to him. You're talking rubbish." She knew.

I think the lead singer from Coldplay was influenced by Dave Berry. I'd like to hear a cover version from Dave of a Coldplay song. It would prove a point and get people talking!

In among all those sixties hit-makers, Dave Berry stood out as an individualist. Dave and I were delighted to work with him on a recording of the Billy Swan song *Queen of my Heart* and one of our own compositions, *I'm A Rocker*.

Bryan Longworth with a 1960s poster of Dave

Bryan Longworth, journalist

IN 1958 I was appointed district editor of what was then the Sheffield area edition of the *South Yorkshire Times* known as the *Woodhouse Express,* initially based in an office in Woodhouse and then in Darnall. I had not been there very long before hearing about a young singer and his group, Dave Berry and The Cruisers, starting to make a name for themselves.

At that time Dave lived with his parents at Robin Lane, Beighton, which was right in the paper's circulation area and after first meeting him I realised that here was a guy who was going to be good for news stories. I called at his home most weeks on my rounds where his mum, Bessie Grundy, always made me feel at home and was very hospitable.

Right from the start I got on extremely well with Dave who had a very good news sense which led to numerous stories for my own paper and for the nationals which I also represented.

Dave told me that he had such big feet that he had to have his shoes specially made by a London shoemaker, which at that time was very unusual and this made a good story and picture for the local press and also the *Daily Mirror*; the first time a piece about him had appeared in a national paper. There was a similar story when a shoe repairer at Woodhouse became Dave's personal cobbler which attracted the headline "Cobbler to King Dave".

With Dave being so popular in Holland I soon found a good market in Dutch newspapers for stories and pictures about him and they regularly paid me in Gilders, sending cash in envelopes through the post which I paid into my account at the then Midland Bank in Woodhouse - a bit of a novelty for the staff there.

When I moved to the Darnall office Dave was a regular caller for plugs for his gigs at Darnall Public Hall in particular and elsewhere. He was a journalist's dream contact, being always good for a story and over the following years I did a succession of items about him as he appeared in the Top Ten and became a big star. My own favourites were *The Crying Game* and *Memphis Tennessee*. It is great to have known him right from the beginning of his musical career and he is still such a nice guy.

Richard Hawley singer/songwriter

Richard Hawley

I FIRST became aware of Dave through my father, Dave Hawley, and my uncle, Frank White, who played with Dave in the Cruisers in the 1960s. Frank was the guy who played the big white double-neck Gibson guitar. They would both always talk of him with the greatest of respect and fondness.

I was made aware of Dave's legendary record collection as well as his own music. It was obvious to me that he had a vast knowledge of really great music from the likes of Chuck Berry to Johnny Burnette. Dave had a copy of the legendary, and at the time, super-rare first rockabilly album of Burnette's which was much coveted in Sheffield music circles.

He was way ahead of the pack at the time and was deeply into American music, being amongst only a tiny handful of Sheffield musicians who were aware of these wonderful records. This gave him a head start on the rest. Dave's interpretation of that music was unique, however, which set him apart from all the others. He is also one of the best live performers this country has ever produced - completely unique.

He is a man I greatly admire; as a fellow Sheffielder I know how hard it is to achieve things in the music industry hailing from here, even nowadays, but Dave did it way before any of us and at a time when it was so, so much more difficult. That was a *massive* achievement and cannot be underestimated.

He has always understood how much the music matters and long may he continue to do so.

Harry Goodwin, Top of the Pops photographer

DAVE Berry was one of the most photogenic celebrities I ever worked with and as Top of the Pops photographer for ten years from 1963, I met the lot. When he arrived on the scene I noticed he had a great face, just like that of a film star, and he has always been a real gentleman too.

I remember the first time I photographed Dave I drove over to meet him at his home in Sheffield in the days before he was married. Although I worked with him on many other occasions, those initial pictures were the best ones I ever took of him.

He knew exactly what to do when I photographed him and I put Dave in the top bracket of performers I have had the pleasure of working with. I am delighted he has kept in touch with me throughout his illustrious career.

As for Dave's records, The Crying Game was a big one for him and I was as thrilled as anyone to see it sell so many copies.

Harry 'Starmaker' Goodwin

Dave with the longest-serving member of The Cruisers, Brian Wood

Brian Wood, Guitarist with The Cruisers

IN my day job running the S21-Live project in Eckington, Derbyshire, I teach music to young people and try to instill in them a similar sense of professionalism to that which Dave Berry has always demonstrated.

Dave certainly has high standards. Being in his band The Cruisers can be demanding at times but we have had some really good times together, we have been to some very special places and we get along pretty well.

I have been a part of Dave's band for more than twenty years, originally joining as bass player when The Cruisers returned to being Sheffield-based; my nephew Jason has been with us as guitarist for seventeen years.

Dave is notorious for changing the set list from show to show, often without giving his musicians any notice at all. On stage I am the link between Dave and the band and he certainly keeps us on our toes.

People turn up to see Dave but the band goes out as a unit and we have a first class attitude and are proud of what we achieve. We treat all shows exactly the same, whether we are performing at a village hall or somewhere like the Chelmsford Festival in front of more than 10,000 people.

We like to retain an excitement in our set and Dave allows us all to express ourselves. He has given me an opportunity to play pedal-steel guitar on tours and we are encouraged to demonstrate our individual talents with guitar solos. Over the years the musical influences of Jason and myself have combined with Dave's own influences and we have enjoyed working together. Dave Berry and The Cruisers never stand still and, even after all this time, if there is something we can improve on, we will strive to do so.

Being a part of The Cruisers has led to me meeting Paul Young, Roger Taylor, Madeleine Bell and many others. Dave is regarded very highly by his fellow performers and when Roger Daltrey came to see us at Truro he told me how much he had enjoyed our show.

I was thrilled to sail on the QE2 for three weeks with Dave during which time I was only asked to work for an hour or two and in 2010 I am looking forward to playing guitar at The Royal Albert Hall; how else would I achieve that without being in The Cruisers?

I once considered teaching Dave how to play guitar but to see him on stage with an instrument in his hand would not have been right. That is not his forte but as a front man everyone knows he is one of the best in the business.

Johnnie Hamp

Johnnie Hamp, former head of entertainment, Granada Television

IN the mid-sixties I produced *Scene at 6.30*, Granada TV's nightly magazine programme. It was my job to present a recording artiste, or group, for every show - The Beatles, The Rolling Stones, The Beach Boys, Sonny and Cher - all the top British and American stars. One of my very favourite performers was Dave Berry who I invited back with every record he released.

Dave had a unique style of presentation in his performance combining his distinctive voice with an understated sexy approach to a song which I know got the girls going, but which didn't stand in the way of his appeal to the rock 'n' rolling lads.

Dave's version of *The Crying Game* is one of my all-time favourites and I have included it in many of the *Desert Island Discs*-type of radio shows on which I have been a guest over the years.

Dave was later to appear for me in many other productions including *The International Pop Proms* where he worked in the company of artistes such as Roy Orbison, Johnny Mathis, Andrew Lloyd Webber and other top international stars.

I recall an instance when we were rehearsing *Scene at 6.30* in the studio. The TV monitors were picking up the rehearsals and broadcasting the pictures to every office in the Granada building. A rather snooty lady production assistant, who usually worked on classical music programmes, burst into my office and screamed out in her perfect cut-glass accent: “Who is that dishy hunk of manhood you have brought in today? Can I go down to the studio to get a closer look?”

It was Dave Berry. I didn't tell Dave about that at the time as I didn't think he'd be particularly interested in Mozart!

The fact that Dave is still around and bringing pleasure to us all after fifty years is a testament to the extraordinary gift he has - a universally popular talent to entertain.

Ray Davies

Ray Davies, The Kinks

WHEN I wrote *This Strange Effect* it certainly wasn’t for The Kinks. We had met Dave Berry at a TV station and I had his voice in mind and I thought it might be nice for him. He had a similar voice, in a way, to the way I sang and he got into the whole mood of the song.

His version had a real atmosphere to it and there are colours in his recording. There was no tangible reason why it was such a success in Holland but it blew one of The Kinks’ own songs out of the chart. The downside was that my band’s record wasn’t a number one, but the consolation was that I had written the song for Dave which got there instead. It was an odd situation to be in.

Chris Spedding, session guitarist

ON Saturday mornings circa 1959/60, there was a "Teenage Show" at The Gaumont Cinema in Sheffield city centre. The shows started with a film, something like The Three Stooges, or a serialised episode of the The Lone Ranger or Hopalong Cassidy, followed by local bands live on stage.

One of the best and most memorable of these bands was Dave Berry and The Cruisers. This was the first professional rock band I ever saw live. I was 15 years old; I've not been the same since. This was a million miles away from the amateur efforts of my own band of school friends, The Vulcans, and our other neighbourhood bands in the suburb of Millhouses.

I particularly remember Dave went on to have a rather special guitarist, Frank White, in his band. Not only was he about the best guitarist I'd heard up until that time who wasn't playing on a record, he had a Stratocaster which, for a young man like me, immediately put him in a class along with Hank Marvin and Buddy Holly!

Chris Spedding

But Dave's performance was brilliant. He had that star quality thing going right from the beginning. Very charismatic and the females in the audience knew it, too, and would call out their pet name for him, "Sugar!"

Even more notable, for 1960, was Dave's repertoire, which leaned so heavily on Chuck Berry. *Sweet Little Sixteen* had already been a UK hit for Chuck but most of us knew very few of the rest of his songs. Dave seemed to know the whole Chuck Berry catalogue and made it his own. He was one the of the earliest UK champions of rhythm 'n' blues, which was to become so influential later in the decade.

It was certainly my first introduction to the full range of Chuck Berry's material. I'd descend on Violet May's famous record shop in Sheffield searching for other American imports. I discovered Muddy Waters, Howling Wolf and Bo Diddley and a whole new world of music opened up. Thanks, Dave!

Later The Vulcans managed to get booked at the Teenage Show and Dave and The Cruisers were topping the bill! An exciting day for us. The Vulcans must have been pretty naff but Dave was very gracious to us all.

The following year I left school and moved down to London to try to break into the music biz, and a few years later, when Dave started getting his hits, I felt very proprietorial: "Oh yes, we knew all about Dave Berry up north – he was always great."

John Firminger, drummer with The Cruisers

ALTHOUGH Sheffield has always very much been Dave's base, Blackpool played an important role in his early years as a performer. It must have been the summer of 1962 when Dave first went there and made a guest appearance at a small club, The Picador, at the side of Blackpool's football ground. Needless to say, the band went down a storm and blew the minds of many of the local musicians who would gravitate to the club.

The following year Dave and the band returned for a two-week stint and had a great time. A number of their loyal followers from Sheffield made the trip for a week's holiday, enjoying the sun and sea in the daytime and their favourite band at night. In one Press interview Dave praised Blackpool as the "guv'nor rave town".

The Picador attracted many other out-of-town musicians who were working in Blackpool in the various theatre shows. These included members of top London band The Fleerekkers who would often call in for an after-hours jam-session. Another young musician was a local 15-year-old pianist called Tony Ashton who had been told about this hot band from Sheffield by his friend Val, who would subsequently go on to marry Cruisers' guitarist, the late Roy Barber. On their way to work together, Val had told Tony all about the band and how they included a number of great Chuck Berry and R&B songs in their set. When he got to meet and play with Dave and Co, it was a marriage made in heaven as the youngster was a natural and brilliant rock 'n' roll pianist. Tony would invariably visit the Picador and sit in with Dave and the band in their sets.

By the early 1990s, Tony Ashton was based in London where Roy and Val Barber recall meeting up with him and being told that one of his greatest disappointments was not being asked to join Dave Berry and The Cruisers back then in Blackpool. Instead he went on to join The Remo Four and subsequently became a highly-respected session player and a member of Ashton, Gardner & Dyke.

Around 1964 The Picador was taken over half-share by the great British rocker Johnny Kidd, whose massive wooden effigy stood looming in front of the club. The venue certainly played its part in Dave's career and gave him plenty of exposure to people from all over the country who were on holiday there.

In November 1963, following one of Dave's frequent gigs at Doncaster Baths, we were visited by Ian Stewart, roadie and pianist with The Rolling Stones. The Stones were also in Doncaster that night on their first nationwide tour as part of a package alongside The Everly Brothers, Little Richard and Bo Diddley. Dave and The Cruisers had met The Stones the previous September when they shared the bill at the Floral Hall, Morecambe, and immediately struck up a friendship through their mutual interest in blues and R&B music.

Ian invited Dave and the band back to the nearby Danum Hotel where The Stones and most of the other tour members were staying. Naturally we were all very excited about possibly seeing some of the stars

John Firminger (third from left) pictured with Dave, fellow Cruisers Carl Baker, Brian Wood, Jason Wood, and another music legend, Van Morrison

and eagerly set off walking round the corner to the Danum. I recall most vividly the broad smile on Brian Jones' face when he saw Dave and the band and likewise with Bill Wyman.

In the hallway I also remember seeing Jerome Green, the legendary maracas player with Bo Diddley and also Bo's female guitarist, "The Duchess". Mick Jagger and Keith Richard seemed a little more aloof as they obviously had other thoughts on their mind with the two young ladies they had in tow. As we talked with Bill and Brian, I soon realised just how much the two bands admired each other as they talked about their recent gigs.

It wasn't long before the door flew open and bursting in came the larger-than-life Little Richard shouting his customary "Well alright, well alright!". I recall how Dave and myself just looked at each other, laughed and shouted "Little Richard!"

Tony Iommi with Dave

Tony Iommi, Black Sabbath

I REMEMBER when I first got to see Dave Berry in the 1960s on TV. He had such a different image to anyone else who was around at that time.

I really liked his voice and the way he moved on stage. The way that he would hold his coat collar up, just peering over it, that was really cool. What a great image in those days and of course he wore all black; I loved it!

Dave has gone on to earn himself a great legacy, is still playing to sell-out gigs to this day and I am pleased to say that he has become one of my very good friends.

Marthy Berry, wife

LIFE with Dave has been a wonderful adventure for the past 45 years or so but things could have turned out differently and I might well have gone off with one of the Everly Brothers instead!

In my home country of Holland I had a friend who was a script-writer and it was through him that I began working in theatres and then alongside TV presenters on game shows. For a time I worked for a promoter who had his own operatic and ballet shows and my role was to book theatres and deal with administration.

I also wrote a short column for a magazine and a highlight came in 1961 when the publication featured me being fired from a cannon at Tony Boltini's circus. Looking back, that was a stupid thing to do but I was carefree and didn't even consider that I could have been seriously injured. Fortunately I only suffered a cut lip when I landed face-first in the net. I moved on to work for some guys who produced commercials with their own film business and through that job I got to know several photographers and people from record companies, including someone from Decca.

Preparing to be fired from a cannon

My boss was filming cinema cigarette advertisements in Knokke at the time of the big Song Festival and a friend took me along in her car. On the second day, we noticed someone from England rehearsing and we both said "God, who is that?" It was Dave and although it was only a rehearsal, he was very impressive indeed. Later, I saw him around doing some interviews but we never met.

Back at work, I asked my boss if he would be able to get me an LP of Dave's because he had been such a success at Knokke and I really liked his music. Then, when I heard that he was to be a special guest at the Grande Gala du Disque in Amsterdam, my friend from Decca said he was taking care of several artists there, including Dave, and that he would be able to get tickets for my friend and I.

We were at the Amstel Hotel and as we picked up our tickets we noticed a crowd of people in the bar, including Dave and Wayne Fontana. We began chatting, got on really well and Dave invited my friend and I to meet him in the hospitality room later. We sat there for ages waiting for him to appear and thought we might as well go home. It was then that one of the Everlys, Phil, asked me out for a drink but even though I was a big fan of theirs I told him I was sorry but I was waiting for someone else. As we reluctantly got up to leave I heard someone shout my name; it was Dave and he wanted to know where I was going to. Dave and Wayne stayed on in Holland for another two nights and my friend and I took them all around Amsterdam.

He said he would telephone me and a week and a half later he did so, inviting me to visit him in Sheffield for a few days. I was due to travel to London to get a film processed for work so decided to catch an evening flight on from there to Manchester and it proved to be a memorable trip. Looking out of the window at the ground beneath us, I couldn't believe my eyes. I told the passenger sitting next to me "I don't want to worry you but I think England is on fire." He laughed out loud before telling me all about the Gunpowder Plot and Bonfire Night celebrations.

Once in Sheffield, a journalist asked if I was Dave's girlfriend and I denied it all, saying I was a friend of his sister's. For a pop star to admit to having a steady girlfriend was not the done thing. We got along so well right from the start. I had always been viewed as slightly eccentric and was never one for being part of the crowd and I could tell Dave was just like me. I didn't feel strange anymore; everything fell into place

Marthy and Dave at their Derbyshire home

and I knew he was the one for me. We did lots of crazy things when we were courting such as rushing off all over Europe at a moment's notice when he was between gigs.

It was good that we met when I was 25 and he was 27, so he had had a chance to get the wild man of rock thing out of his blood and I wasn't a young, impressionable girl any more. Dave proposed on a flight to Spain and when I said "yes" he produced a ring there and then which was very romantic. We went out for two years before getting married and now, when I look back, I can hardly believe it. Not only was I marrying a rock star with a huge following, I was leaving my home and all my friends for a country where I knew no-one.

I used to travel quite a lot with Dave, but not always. I didn't feel I had to keep my eye on him as I am not a jealous person and I think that has gone a long way towards keeping us together. He is the romantic type, more in a thoughtful way than a sickly one. We share the same sense of humour, have the same standards and know what we like and dislike in other people.

I admire Dave's professionalism and his enthusiasm for a job which also happens to be his hobby. Occasionally I might ask him if something he is doing is absolutely necessary and he will tell me "I just want to do it right".

In the late 1970s Dave worked with a band from Birmingham for a short time and one of them wanted help with a radio jingle he was doing. Dave told him that I could sing harmonies so I agreed to help out. When he heard me he said "Oh, you *can* sing harmonies" and soon afterwards recruited me on stage to join The Cruisers. I've continued to appear with the band on and off and really enjoy it because it gives me a purpose at some of the shows.

When Tania was born, Dave was a very good father. Although he was often away working at night, he was also around for much of the daytime. At school Tania hated the fact that her dad was famous. Other kids would tell her they had seen his picture in the papers and she often asked why he couldn't have an ordinary job, like being a postman.

It has been a very exciting life and a wonderful journey, meeting lovely people and visiting beautiful places. Dave and I are a team and we know each other inside out. I have put up with a lot from his fans and maybe at times I was stupid not to worry about him but I never did and he has rewarded the trust I placed in him. I am his number one fan. And I can't believe he has let me have the last word in his book!

Relaxing with our daughter Tania and granddaughter Mariella

Index